MYTHOLOGY

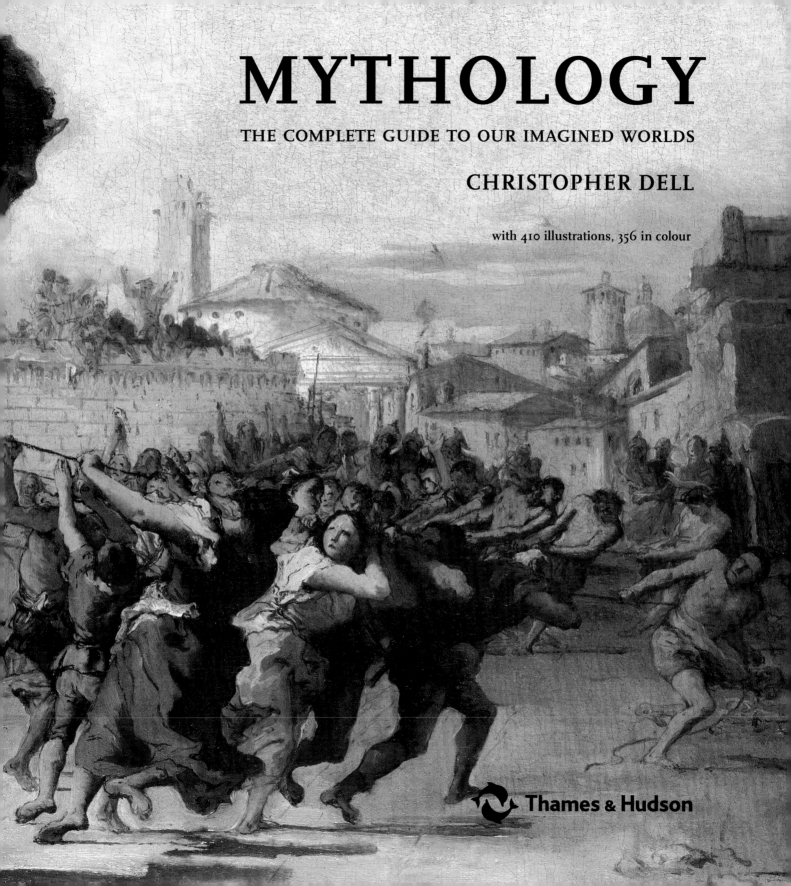

MYTHOLOGY

THE COMPLETE GUIDE TO OUR IMAGINED WORLDS

CHRISTOPHER DELL

with 410 illustrations, 356 in colour

Thames & Hudson

CONTENTS

IIIIIIIIIIIIIIIIIIIIIIIIIIIIIIIIIIIIIIIIIIIIIIIIIIIIIIII

HALF-TITLE A 19th-century illustration of a seer discovering Asgard, the home of the Nordic gods.
TITLE PAGE Giovanni Domenico Tiepolo, *The Procession of the Trojan Horse into Troy*, c. 1760. National Gallery, London.
OPPOSITE (left to right) An ancient Sumerian sculpture of a bull's head, 3rd millennium BC; a Zapotec mask of a god, Mexico, 150 BC – AD 100; a double-headed serpent, Mexico, 15th–16th centuries AD.

First published in the United Kingdom in 2012 by
Thames & Hudson Ltd, 181A High Holborn, London WC1V 7QX

British Library Cataloguing-in-Publication Data
A catalogue record for this book is available from the British Library

ISBN 978-0-500-51615-7

Printed and bound in China by C & C Offset Printing Co. Ltd

To find out about all our publications, please visit
www.thamesandhudson.com.
There you can subscribe to our e-newsletter, browse or download our current catalogue, and buy any titles that are in print.

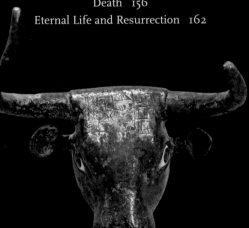

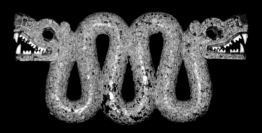

INTRODUCTION

|||||||||||||||||||||||||||||||||||||||||||||||||||||||||||||||||||||||||||||||||||||||||||||||||

'Myth is the foundation of life; it is the timeless pattern, the pious formula, into which life flows when it reproduces its traits out of the unconscious.'

THOMAS MANN

The desire to tell stories is a fundamental part of the human condition. When it is coupled with an innate need to make sense of our surroundings and to understand the origins of things, the result is mythology. This is not to say that humankind is the primary focus of myths: rather, their true attraction lies in vivid, fantastical gods that create worlds, shape mountains, arrange stars and fill oceans. After creating the scenery, they set about populating it with humans and other animals, granting mankind the gifts of civilization and laying down the basic natural laws of our world.

That these stories are universal and timeless is evident from our continuing interest in mythology. Generation after generation relishes the stories of Theseus' battle with the Minotaur, Gilgamesh's heroic exploits or the events narrated in the great Indian *Mahabharata*. Thor stars in Hollywood films, and the legend of King Arthur has spawned an entire industry. One reason behind this interest is that mythologies brim with very human emotions: love and hate, bravery and foolishness, wickedness and goodness. D. H. Lawrence described myth as 'an attempt to narrate a whole human experience, of which the purpose is too deep, going too deep in the blood and soul, for mental explanation or description'.

As Lawrence suggests, myths are rarely just a form of entertainment. They are more urgent, more important than mere narrative: they embody elements that take humanity back to its origins. An important part of mythology is cosmogony, or an explanation of how the universe came into existence. Like the Old Testament, which opens with the words 'In the beginning', most mythologies conceive of a time when the world did not exist, of disorder before order. Myths attempt to explain basic concepts such as the existence of good and evil, the (apparent) movement of the sun,

OPPOSITE *The stars are closely associated with mythology. These strange beings relate to signs of the zodiac.* ABOVE *The myth of Pandora explains how humans came to be human, with all of our flaws.*

the changing of the seasons and the differences between the sexes, and local myths are invoked to account for the origins of mountains and rivers. One of the earliest surviving mythological texts, the *Epic of Gilgamesh*, offers insights into such arcane subjects as why snakes shed their skin and why meat left outside becomes putrid.

At the heart of all myths lies the notion of a supernatural realm that somehow guards some greater knowledge – the truth, perhaps, of how and why we arrived here. Man is admitted only rarely to this supernatural world, which is the preserve of gods. These gods are central to the world's mythologies, calling the universe into existence and often forming men with their own hands. The Greek philosopher Xenophanes argued in the 5th century BC that all beings create gods in their own image; the gods of Greek mythology certainly demonstrate decidedly human behaviour, with their squabbles, petty jealousies and ill-advised love affairs.

It is important to remember, however, that the Greek gods – like all others – also served an important religious function, even if that role seems obscure and distant to us today. The distinction between myth and religion is a fine one, but cannot be ignored. 'Mythology is what we call someone else's religion,' wrote Joseph Campbell, an American scholar who made comparative religion his life's work. Mark Twain described the Bible as 'a mass of fables and traditions, mere mythology'. The 19th-century Scottish biblical scholar William Robertson Smith sought to distinguish between ancient and modern religion, viewing modern religion as built on belief, but ancient religion as based on ritual. In fact, the relationship is rather more complicated, but it could be argued that 'religion' implies a wholehearted belief in a particular set of stories or events that have been approved by an authority or even divinely ordained. From this core of stories springs ritual, which keeps the stories alive, reinforcing key points of the belief in the minds of believers.

Perhaps the distinction between religion and mythology can best be summed up by describing the religion of today as the mythology of tomorrow. After all, the ancient Greeks worshipped and sacrificed to their gods, while the stories that had sprung up around them contained moral messages central to the running of society. What makes people able to believe passionately in one set of mythologies while rejecting another out of hand is simply part of what makes us human. Any book on mythology will discuss elements of living religions, including Buddhism,

ABOVE *The hero Theseus, son of Poseidon, straddles the divide between mortal and divine. Here he is visiting the underwater palace of Amphitrite (seated).* BELOW *Xolotl, the Aztec god of death who guided souls to the underworld.*

Christianity, Islam and Hinduism, not to mention a range of North American Indian beliefs and a variety of local folklores (for example, in Japan, China, Korea and Australia) that are still widely followed. It is important to note that discussion of such beliefs in the context of mythology does not suggest that they are untrue, but simply that in many ways they reflect broader themes – themes that may say something important about human nature. Good examples are the stories of self-sacrifice, virgin birth, saints, dragons and demons that appear to be universally common. To miss out important aspects of living religions would be to present an incomplete picture.

This book differs from many other surveys of mythology by considering all of the major mythological traditions side by side: Celtic, Greco-Roman, Norse, Buddhist, Oriental, Native American, Central and South American, Near Eastern and African. Sometimes these convenient categories hide many (potentially conflicting) strands: the three 'Oriental' mythologies of China, Japan and Korea differ from each other in key areas, while the term 'African' groups together hundreds of distinct traditions. Similarly, while Roman mythology is clearly based on Greek mythology, it is often more complicated than simply substituting Jupiter for Zeus and Diana for Artemis.

ABOVE *This Egyptian amulet of the Eye of Horus suggests that humans make gods in their own image.* BELOW *The night sky contains the outline of various mythological stories.*

Since mythologies address our most fundamental experiences, different mythological traditions frequently overlap. Myths were also spread by conquest and trade. Much has been written, for example, on the way Celtic mythology developed from broader Indo-European culture, and it is also true that the Celts rarely produced images of their gods until they came under Roman influence. Because of these connections, this book is arranged by theme rather than by culture, which will allow the reader to make comparisons. Instead of following the myths' development chronologically, it explores recurring motifs as they appear around the world, from the significance of symbolic substances – blood, for example – to the way in which different mythologies have explained our origins.

That there are certain striking similarities between different mythological traditions has inevitably led some scholars to assume that they shared a common origin, be it cultural or psychological. As early as the 19th century, writers were beginning to look more closely at these common elements, even if their conclusions were sometimes tailored

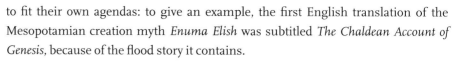

ABOVE *The Great Flood (here we see Noah in his ark) is an archetypal myth found in many different cultures.* BELOW *The Egyptian god Thoth in the guise of a baboon teaches humanity how to write.*

to fit their own agendas: to give an example, the first English translation of the Mesopotamian creation myth *Enuma Elish* was subtitled *The Chaldean Account of Genesis*, because of the flood story it contains.

The concept of the archetype – the recurring motif, the universal story – is therefore of central importance. J. P. Frazer's *The Golden Bough*, which first appeared in 1890, is widely recognized as the breakthrough work in this field. A publishing phenomenon when it first arrived in bookshops, it soon fell out of favour among academics who had reservations about Frazer's methods. Nevertheless, his painstaking analysis of hundreds of myths and beliefs around the world laid the groundwork for future generations of students and encouraged a more scientific and anthropological approach to the subject. (Interestingly, the work caused some scandal when it was first published, since it dared to include a discussion of Christ alongside various more 'primitive' religions, effectively 'relegating' Christianity to the status of myth.) The psychoanalyst Carl Jung also investigated myths as possible reflections of a collective unconscious shared between humans.

Yet the most often cited work in the field of comparative mythology is Joseph Campbell's *The Hero with a Thousand Faces* (1949). In this highly influential book Campbell explored the idea that all heroic myths have a common ancestor, which he dubbed the 'monomyth', effectively laying out the path of every hero. Today this approach has fallen out of fashion, but the fact remains that mythology undeniably has certain common tropes. Some are readily explicable: the symbolic importance of blood in Aztec, Christian and South African San cultures is easily explained by the fact that blood runs in all our veins. But what are we to make of the similarities between Noah's Flood and the deluges associated with Deucalion and Gilgamesh? In each case a divine being or beings viewed mankind as sinful or irritating and decided to wipe them out. The rainbow is a remarkable phenomenon that in ancient times demanded, and yet defied, simple explanation. Gold seems to have fascinated people all over the world. Stories of virgin births are found frequently, and twins are often endowed with special significance. Sibling rivalry appears and reappears. Perhaps this tells us that myths are simply daily life raised to heroic levels. After all, who has not fallen out with a brother or sister?

We should not overlook the political or pragmatic value of mythology. The *Kalevala* mythic cycle was first compiled only in the 19th century, in order to shore up Finnish nationalism. The Yoruba of Nigeria today still invoke the *itan* – a collective noun embracing mythology, religious beliefs, songs and history – to resolve disputes.

This is where mythology becomes very real. Some may see the Old Testament story of Noah's Ark as being purely mythological, while others regard it as literal truth.

Just as with religion, however, there is rarely total orthodoxy. For example, Greek mythology includes more than one account of humanity's beginnings. The sequence of events shifts with each retelling, a continual reinvention. Mesopotamian mythology, which developed over a period of perhaps two millennia, similarly varied over time, giving precedence to particular gods in particular cities. In China and Japan we find a constant blurring of myth and historical fact – and, in fact, early historians in those countries made no distinction between the two. They refer to emperors who almost certainly existed, yet many of the feats ascribed to them are unlikely to have occurred.

Many centuries later, Christians looked in pagan myths for signs of their own religion. Norse myths clearly incorporate elements of Christian myth – and in English, at least, provided a name for the Christian underworld (from the Norse goddess Hel). Although we attempt to divide myths into neat, self-contained traditions, the truth is that they are, or at least were, constantly evolving and inter-mingling. One of the most intriguing examples is the tradition whereby the wind gods in Japan are typically depicted carrying wind bags: the same motif is found in ancient Greek mythology and almost certainly arrived in the Far East via the conquests of Alexander the Great. A good idea that seized the imagination could linger long in the mind.

ABOVE *This imagining of the Norse mythological universe has been pieced together from various sources. There is rarely much orthodoxy in mythologies.* BELOW *Our understanding of Celtic mythology comes mostly from such items as the Iron Age Gundestrup Cauldron.*

Adding to the confusion is the fact that different mythologies are documented to varying degrees. In the case of Classical mythology, we have a vast range of written and artistic sources, but Mesopotamian mythology exists in scattered texts. Despite the huge volume of arte-facts to have survived from thousands of years of ancient Egyptian culture, we know very little about its mythology, and what we do know comes mostly from much later Greek and Roman sources. Celtic mythology is perhaps the most opaque, since almost no texts or inscriptions survive, and we depend on Irish and Welsh myths to give us a flavour of what was once a pan-European culture. African mythology remains similarly obscure, reliant as it is almost entirely on oral traditions. Our understanding of Norse myth – the stories of Thor and Odin, the Midgard Serpent and Valhalla – is almost entirely dependent on the 13th-century *Poetic* and *Prose Eddas* compiled by the Icelandic writer Snorri Sturluson from oral tradition.

What of myths in the present day? Is there a place for new myths, or do we live in a society too dominated by science? Archaeologists two thousand years from now may conclude that one of the most significant myths of the late 20th and early 21st centuries was *Star Wars*; its characters were immortalized in small figurines, and countless books detailed their exploits. Moreover, they will find evidence of these stories worldwide. Archaeologists may even come to the conclusion that the narrative falls into canonical and non-canonical parts.

Such apparently idle musings hide an important point. George Lucas has made it clear that one of the major influences on *Star Wars* was Campbell's *The Hero With a Thousand Faces*. And *Star Wars* in fact features many of the archetypes that are discussed in this book: twins separated at birth, redemption, self-sacrifice, quests, a clash between good and evil, hidden cities, secrets and – of course – a whole host of monsters for the hero or heroes to despatch at regular intervals. There is also a gradual revelation of knowledge, as the hero, Luke Skywalker, comes to terms with his destiny, eventually slaying his father and fulfilling a prophecy.

The present book is divided into eight sections that explore what makes myths so interesting for us. It begins with a survey of the supernatural realm – fundamental to all types of mythology – examining its origins, the various types of beings that inhabit it, and how it interacts with the human world. (This relationship is essential to mythology, since it is the supernatural element that introduces the magic and unpredictability that make myths so appealing.)

The second chapter looks at how mythology has been used to explain the world's geography and topology. Human beings are central to the next two sections, which explore stories relating to our origins and development. There follows a chapter on the important role of animals in myth, and one on symbolic materials, objects and substances. (It is fascinating to see how the same substances take on different meanings in diverse cultures.) The final two chapters look in more depth at heroes of mythology, and at some of their key quests.

This book looks at mythology principally through its images, which are gathered from around the world. Sometimes they are contemporary with the beliefs they portray – ancient Greek vases, Mesopotamian figurines, medieval manuscripts, Chinese silk paintings – and sometimes they are much later. This is in keeping with the nature of mythology, which, as a quick look at the number of books published on the subject shows us, is very much a living thing. It is fascinating to see manuscripts from the Middle Ages depicting scenes from ancient mythology, which illustrates myth's lasting power to inspire; stories are recited and reinvented, in the process adding an extra layer of magic to our day-to-day existence.

OPPOSITE *Yama, the Buddhist Lord of Death, grips the Wheel of Life; its six sections represent the realms of the gods, the titans, humans, animals, the hungry ghosts and the demons.* ABOVE *The Hindu god Hanuman carries a mountain to his dying master.* BELOW *The Burmese version of Vishnu, shown riding on his mount, Garuda.*

1

THE
SUPERNATURAL
REALM

At the heart of all world mythologies lies a belief in a supernatural realm, beyond our earthbound day-to-day lives. This 'other world' typically predates humankind and is the source of all being, animating the universe and giving our existence meaning. It is this supernatural realm that gives birth to the gods, monsters and magic that together form the basis of every mythology.

Almost all mythologies are concerned with cosmology – where our universe comes from, how it originated, and even how it might end. In most mythologies the universe is divided into various tiers. Typically there are three: the realm of the gods (often known as 'heaven'); the earth, where humans live; and some sort of underworld (often known as 'hell'). In many early traditions – particularly Mesopotamian and Greek – these levels were born from Chaos, the universe in its primordial state, and were fashioned from the gods themselves. In Greek myth, for example, the sky was known as Aether, the earth as Gaia, and the underworld as Tartarus – names that stood both for gods and for places. Other mythologies added extra layers: in the Nordic stories, for example, there are nine worlds, arranged around a giant tree, Yggdrasil. The Yoruba of Nigeria, on the other hand, simply distinguish between physical (*aiye*) and invisible (*orun*) worlds.

The universe's upper and lower layers are generally inhabited by gods and inaccessible to humans (at least while they are alive). Pantheons of gods are common to almost all mythologies: in most cases there are stories relating how one god became more powerful than the others, through brute strength, trickery or superior intellect. In ancient Greece this was Zeus (known to the Romans as Jupiter); in Norse mythology, Odin. For the ancient Mesopotamians (who lived in an area roughly corresponding to modern-day Iraq),

PRECEDING PAGES *The division of the universe into distinct realms is clearly seen in this painting of the Assumption by Francesco Botticini.* OPPOSITE *Zeus, leader of the Greek gods, brandishes his thunderbolts.* ABOVE AND RIGHT *The heavens are almost always barred to humans. Here, Icarus and Phaethon fall to earth after attempting to fly.*

their chief god varied from city to city, though they essentially shared a common mythology.

The inferior gods still had many important roles to play, however. Often there are many such gods – the Aztecs, for example, had hundreds, each with a different function. Almost all pantheons include figures who relate to basic human needs: love, fertility, music, art, rainfall, childbirth and farming, as well as war.

Many gods have decidedly human traits. They are jealous, even petty and squabbling. Siblings fall out (as was the case with Zeus and his brothers), children rebel against their parents, and some monstrous parents devour their children. From time to time, one or more minor deities may decide to challenge the chief god's authority, leading to a battle in the heavens. (For most gods, war and conflict are everyday occurrences.) Even in monotheistic Christianity, God was challenged by the angel Satan, who was punished by being cast down to hell.

Alongside the gods are other beings, sometimes themselves divine, who play the role of tricksters. Coyote in Native American Indian tales, Loki in Norse myth and Maui in the Polynesian traditions are all examples of unpredictable characters who sometimes help and sometimes hinder, but often bring light relief to mythological stories.

More dangerous are the monsters, emblems of untamed chaos: the Norse gods, to give one example, are constantly battling against the Ice Giants. However, in most cases the gods overcome these destabilizing elements (often with the help of heroes), and order is re-established. In addition, almost all mythologies contain creatures that are not quite deities, not quite human. They represent the tail end of the divine spark, and include nymphs, demons, angels, giants, dwarves, spirits, trolls, dryads, fairies and so forth. To this list can be added such beings as the Classical Muses, to whom artists turned when seeking inspiration, or the Fates.

As well as housing gods, the heavens also hold the sun, moon and stars. Greek mythology explains that the stars are the immortalized remains of minor divinities and humans, while the sun is personified as Helios in his chariot, and the moon as Selene. The Aztecs worshipped the sun, the bringer of life, as the god Tonatiuh, who reigned as king of heaven. The solar deity, often symbolized by a golden disk, is understandably common to many cosmologies, from the Sól of Germanic legend to the Hindu god Surya and several ancient Egyptian gods.

Humans, noting the apparent movement of the stars and the phases of the moon, studied the planets to make sense of the universe and even to foretell the future. They also looked to the heavens to explain climatic phenomena. Storm gods are seen as particularly powerful: Thor in Norse mythology, Zeus in Greek, Indra in Hindu, Shango in Yoruba and Taranis in Celtic. For the Native Americans, thunder is caused by the Thunderbird beating its wings. And in China, Lei Gong creates thunder with a drum and a mallet.

The opposite of the storm is the rainbow, which in most mythologies is seen as a sign of peace or as a bridge. Hindu legend views it as the bow of Indra, used to fire bolts of lightning. The *Epic of Gilgamesh*, meanwhile, describes it as the necklace of the Great Mother Ishtar, worn in memory of the Great Flood that had destroyed humanity; and in the Old Testament it signals God's covenant with man, again made after the Flood. To ancient Greeks it was the bridge of Iris, which linked earth and heaven, while in Norse mythology it is known as Bifröst, connecting the worlds of Asgard (heaven) and Midgard (earth). In a sense, the rainbow is the perfect metaphor for all mythology: a mental connection between our mundane surroundings and the mysterious workings of celestial powers.

LEFT *Popular deities travelled between cultures. Cybele was originally a Phrygian earth goddess, but she was adopted by the Romans.* ABOVE *Figurine of Baal, a Near Eastern storm god, found in Ugarit, Syria.* OPPOSITE *Shango is the Yoruba thunder god. His power is symbolized by the carving's axe shape.*

Out of Chaos

All creation myths attempt to explain what came before the stable universe of planets and stars we know today. The answer in many cases is Chaos – a time when the physical matter of the universe was undifferentiated and confused.

In Chinese mythology the universe began as a formless vapour cloud that was transformed into the dualities of *yin* and *yang*. Later myths situate the vapour inside a giant egg; in the centre of this formlessness slept Pan Gu, the creator. One day he smashed the egg open, the lighter parts flying upwards to create the heavens, the darker parts sinking to form the earth.

The story of Pan Gu is related to the Hindu myth of Brahma emerging from a golden egg to create the world. For the ancient Egyptians, meanwhile, the waters of Chaos were separated into the sky, the earth and the underworld.

The word *chaos* comes from ancient Greek, and refers to the empty, unformed state of the early universe. According to Hesiod's *Theogony*, written *c.* 700 BC, Chaos gave birth to Gaia (the earth), Eros (desire), Erebos (darkness), Nyx (night) and Tartarus (the underworld). These in turn engendered the universe's other fundamental building blocks, including Uranus (the heavens), Aether (the sky) and day. Another version of the creation story tells of a goddess, born spontaneously from Chaos, who then laid the egg from which everything hatched. In Mesopotamia, Marduk overcomes the monstrous Tiamat – a personification of chaos – to establish order and human society.

Disorder remains at the fringes, however. The Egyptian god Ra, for example, does daily battle with the chaos serpent Apep, while Mount Olympus, home of the Greek gods, was attacked by the unruly Giants.

BELOW LEFT *The Chinese proto-god Pan Gu turned chaos into order.*
BELOW *The Egyptian god Ptah forms the world-egg on a potter's wheel.*
OPPOSITE *This medieval French manuscript shows the biblical God bringing order to chaos through geometry.*

ABOVE *Bernard Picart's depiction of the primordial chaos, swirling with astrological signs.*
OPPOSITE *Giants – creatures of chaos – pile up rocks in order to storm Mount Olympus.*

The Pantheons

Most mythological systems are polytheistic and feature a pantheon of many gods. A first god typically gives birth to other deities, who then procreate (often incestuously) to spawn new generations. Gradually tasks are distributed, with different gods taking responsibility for the sea, for war, for fertility, for the sun or the moon, and so on.

The core pantheon of ancient Greek mythology, for example – the gods known as the 'Olympians', since they lived on Mount Olympus – includes twelve main deities (Zeus, Hera, Poseidon, Demeter, Athena, Dionysus, Apollo, Artemis, Ares, Aphrodite, Hephaestus and Hermes), plus hundreds of minor gods and demigods. The Mesopotamian pantheon varies from city to city, though certain gods – for example Marduk and Enlil – are universal. The Egyptian pantheon, too, changed according to the preference of pharaohs, though the central triad of Osiris, Isis and Horus remained.

The main Norse gods are known as the Aesir, and include Odin, Thor, Freyr, Idunn and Heimdallr, among almost one hundred others. The Hindu pantheon revolves around three key gods, Brahma, Vishnu and Shiva (see p. 30), but extends to hundreds of minor deities, called *deva*s and *devi*s.

Though their powers are superhuman, most gods take on human form (and often human failings). Some have alternate forms: Hindu gods can have many avatars, while the gods of ancient Mexico or South America appear both in human form and in a variety of animal or plant guises. The same is true of Native American Indian gods and Australian Aboriginal gods, whose pantheon varies hugely from tribe to tribe.

OPPOSITE *The Greek pantheon took its pleasures seriously. This gathering on Olympus resembles a family reunion.* ABOVE *Arrayed ranks of Tibetan animal gods, each responsible for a different aspect of life.*

Deities from Norse mythology: at the back, the sun, the moon,
Tuisco and Seater; at the front, Frigg, Odin and Thor.

Enthroned Egyptian deities, from the temple at Abu Simbel.

OPPOSITE *The pantheon of Hindu gods, goddesses and demons decorates Sri Mariamman Temple, Singapore.* ABOVE *This Japanese domestic shrine brings together sixty-six Shinto and Buddhist gods.*

The Supreme Being

In almost all pantheons a leader god eventually emerges. In the case of Mesopotamian myth, this was Marduk, who reigned after slaying the monster Tiamat. Similarly, the Canaanite god Baal gained power by overcoming the giant Yamm and the sea dragon Lotan.

Heaven is not, however, a democracy, and often the principal god comes to power by force. Zeus, for example, was just one more of Cronus and Rhea's children, alongside Poseidon, Hera and Hades. Cronus, fearing that his children would overthrow him, swallowed them all at birth. However, when the time came for Zeus to be eaten, Rhea deceived Cronus by giving him a stone wrapped in a blanket. The real Zeus grew up elsewhere, one day confronting and overthrowing his father, and retrieving his siblings. Thereafter Zeus was the uncontested king of heaven, while his father was confined to Tartarus (see p. 73).

Almost all supreme beings are male, bearded and associated with thunder. Into this pattern fall the Norse god Odin, his son Thor, Marduk – and also the storm-loving God of the Old Testament. The Hindu situation is a little different: all Hindu gods are effectively an expression of a single genderless supreme force, Brahman, but in reality there are three principal gods, Brahma, Vishnu and Shiva – the Creator, the Sustainer and the Destroyer – together known as the *Trimurti*.

BELOW LEFT *This famous 'sun stone' found in Mexico City shows the Aztec calendar. At the centre is Tonatiuh, who presided over heaven.*
BELOW AND OPPOSITE *Brahma, the Hindu god of creation, is traditionally shown with four heads.*

·IVPITER·

REGIONES
Arabia felix, Celtica, Dalmat. Hispa-
nia, Misnia, Tyrrhenia, Ungaria.
CIVITATES
Auerna, Buda, Cafconia, Matina,
Narbona, Toletum, Volaterra.

Iupiter alatis aquilis per fidera vectus:
Quippe aquilis femper gaudet Deus ille corufc:
Quem Inuenis nudo formatus mollior arcu
Præcedit, fubeunt Pifces: dominatur opaco

Euphrati, Afyrijs, Cilicum campeftribus aris,
Pannoniæ, Calabris, extremifq́s æquore Iberis.
Hic membris tribuit neruos, et acuniá cordi,
Et regale caput, nec delaſſabile pectus.

REGIONES
Calabria, Cilicia, Garamantes, Lydia,
Normandia, Pamphilia, Portugalia.
CIVITATES.
Alexandria, Compoſtella, Hiſpalis, Parm-
tiú, Ratiſbona, Rhotmagun, Vormatia.

The rule of Zeus (Jupiter) went practically unchallenged in Classical
mythology. His power is symbolized by the thunderbolts he wields.

LEFT *Uranus (known to the Romans as Saturn) devours his son Poseidon. His last child, Zeus, escaped this fate and overthrew his father.* BELOW *Michelangelo's image of the biblical God is bearded, elderly and stern.*

Mother Goddesses

Goddesses in mythology are often closely connected with fertility. One of the oldest examples is the 'Willendorf Venus' – a small sculpture made 20,000 years ago that celebrates female reproductive power. Early Egyptian and Western Asian myths also feature powerful fertility figures: the Mesopotamian goddess Ishtar (also known as Inanna) delighted in seduction, while the Phrygian Cybele (also worshipped as the 'Great Mother') presided over the fertility of the land.

In China the great mother goddess is Nuwa, wife of the emperor-god Fuxi. Able to transform herself into a serpent, she created the first humans, using yellow clay for the aristocracy and earth for the rest. The Aztec deity Coatlicue, dressed in a skirt of snakes, gave birth to many gods, who eventually murdered her (though her youngest son, Huitzilopochtli, avenged her).

The Hindu goddess Devi represents the 'divine feminine' and as such forms a female counterpart to the *Trimurti* (see p. 30). She appears in various guises, such as Ma, the mother, and Kali, the destroyer. As goddess of marriage, Zeus' wife, Hera, remained faithful in the face of her husband's infidelities, even if she persecuted her love rivals mercilessly. But we notice her importance subsiding over time, perhaps reflecting a shift from an agricultural society that valued fertility to a society based on war and conquest.

RIGHT *The Aztec mother goddess Coatlicue wearing her skirt of interlaced snakes.* OPPOSITE *A fresco from Pompeii showing the Egyptian mother goddess Isis welcoming Io to Egypt. Hera, jealous of her husband's interest in the Greek nymph, forced Io to roam the world ceaselessly.*

BELOW *Ishtar, as depicted in a terracotta relief from the 2nd millennium* BC, *was a powerful Mesopotamian fertility goddess.*

OPPOSITE RIGHT *The original beings of Chinese mythology, Fuxi and Nuwa, are here intertwined. Nuwa holds a compass, while Fuxi brandishes a carpenter's square.*
BELOW *This image from Athanasius Kircher's* Oedipus Aegyptiacus *shows Isis as a universal mother goddess.* RIGHT *Hera, Zeus' wife and mother to several of the Greek gods.*

Where the Gods Live

Since the gods belong to the supernatural realm, they almost always live apart from humanity. In Hindu, Buddhist and Jain mythology, Brahma lives on Mount Meru, at the centre of the universe. Meru is not an earthly mountain, however, but a miraculous peak said to be 84,000 *yohanas* (about one million kilometres) high. The sun god, Surya, circles it daily.

Taoist philosophy expresses the concept of heaven with the word *tian*, which means simply 'sky'; and this worship of the heavens is commemorated in the famous Temple of Heaven in Beijing. The Japanese heaven is connected to earth by a floating bridge. Both traditions also claim that gods live in mountains made of gold and silver.

The ancient Mesopotamian *Enuma Elish* text suggests that heaven had two layers: the realm of Anu and the realm of Enlil. In Norse mythology humans lived in Midgard, while the Aesir gods lived in Asgard, at the centre of which was Odin's hall, Valhalla.

Descriptions of the Christian heaven are vague, though it is known to be populated by angels. Perhaps the most famous holy abode, however, is Mount Olympus. The tallest mountain in Greece, it was a fitting home for the twelve main gods of ancient Greek mythology.

FAR LEFT *The Christian heaven is inhabited by the Trinity (God, Christ and the Holy Spirit) and hosts of angels.* LEFT *The Temple of Heaven in Beijing.* OPPOSITE *The Norse universe is divided into nine distinct levels, including the realm of fire, Muspelheim (1), and Midgard (3), where humans dwell.*

ABOVE *This Tibetan mural shows a cosmic mandala centred on the world mountain, Meru.* OPPOSITE *A Jain cosmological plan showing the continents where mortals live, separated by ring-like oceans. At the very centre is Mount Meru, at whose summit lives Brahma, the god of creation.*

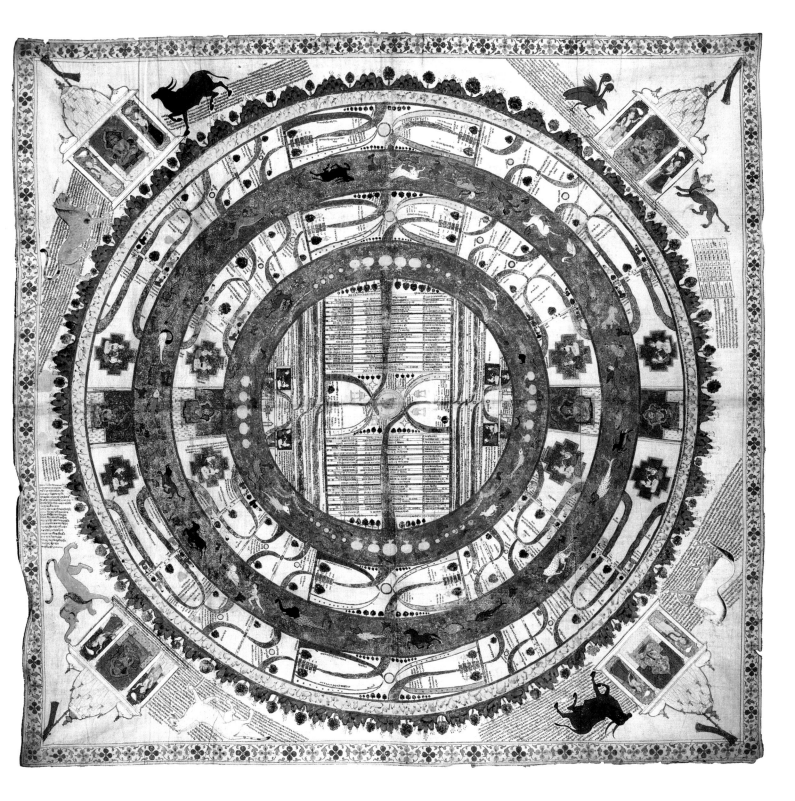

The Sun

Source of warmth and light, marker of the daytime, the sun is central to all mythologies. Its predictable procession across the sky led many cultures to conclude that some being was controlling its movement. For the Egyptians it sailed in a barge, while the Greeks and Northern Europeans imagined it transported on a solar chariot.

For the Greeks and Romans, this chariot was driven by the god Helios (Sol), who lived in the east. Helios' mortal son, Phaethon, demanded permission to drive the chariot. Though Helios tried to dissuade him, Phaethon insisted, but the horses proved too strong for him, and he was thrown to earth. Later Greek mythology associated the sun with Apollo.

For the Egyptians, the sun represented order and was associated with Ra. Every night, the sun passed through the underworld, where it had to fight off attackers, including Apep, the chaos snake.

Central American societies were dominated by sun worship. Huitzilopochtli, an Aztec sun god, had to be fed with human sacrifices. For the Aztecs, the sun was the offspring of the earth, Coatlicue. Some Chinese myths know the sun as the left eye of Pan Gu (see p. 20). In Persian mythology the solar deities are Ahura Mazda and Mithra, both powerful gods.

Eclipses had cosmic significance. For the Chinese, they were the result of the sun being devoured by a dragon. The Egyptians, on the other hand, viewed them as a sign that the sun had momentarily lost its fight against Apep. For the Japanese, an eclipse was a reminder of when the Shinto sun goddess Amaterasu fled to a cave, plunging the world into darkness; happily she was coaxed out again by curiosity, when she heard the other gods laughing. Norse mythology predicts that the sun – the goddess Sól – will eventually be devoured by the wolf Fenrir, possibly during the apocalyptic events of Ragnarok.

BELOW *The sun goddess Amaterasu emerges from her cave, dazzling the other gods.* OPPOSITE *A Persian depiction of the sun, with rays emerging from his head.*

Sol

OPPOSITE LEFT *Phaethon, unable to control his father's horses, falls to earth.* OPPOSITE ABOVE *Apollo travels through the sky.* OPPOSITE BELOW *The sun god Sol rides his chariot.* ABOVE *Solar chariots appear around the world. Here, the red-faced charioteer Aruna drives Surya, the Hindu sun god.*

*Altar showing Selene against a crescent moon,
flanked by either the Dioscuri or Phosphoros (the
Morning Star) and Hesperos (the Evening Star).*

The Moon

Whereas the sun is typically male, the moon is often depicted as female. In Aztec mythology Coyolxauhqui, a daughter of Coatlicue, the earth goddess, attempted to overthrow her mother. However, one of her brothers, Huitzilopochtli, decapitated Coyolxauhqui and tossed her head into the heavens, where it became the moon.

In Greek mythology the moon was originally associated with the Titan Selene, sister of Helios. Perhaps the most famous myth about Selene relates how she fell in love with the shepherd Endymion and asked Zeus to put him into an eternal sleep so that she could appreciate his beauty. Over time, Selene was gradually replaced by Artemis as the moon goddess.

In Mesopotamia, the moon, called Suen (sometimes Sin or Nanna), was the son of Enlil and Ninlil. Some myths tell that Suen was the father of Ishtar. In ancient Egyptian mythology the two gods associated with the moon were Khonsu and the god of magic, Thoth. Numerous traditions, including Native American, make reference to the Moon Rabbit, a shape suggested by marks on the moon's surface. For the Chinese, this figure is mixing the elixir of eternal life in the company of the moon goddess Chang'e. For the Aztecs, he had been put there by Quetzalcoatl to commemorate a rabbit who had sacrificed himself to the god.

ABOVE *Stone disk depicting Coyolxauhqui's dismembered body.*
BELOW *This impression from a Babylonian cylinder seal shows a priest before the symbols of Ishtar (a star) and Suen (the moon).*

ABOVE *The Moon Rabbit mixing the elixir of eternal life with the moon goddess Chang'e.* OPPOSITE *Like the sun, the moon often travels by chariot. Here Selene crosses the night sky in hers.*

The Stars

Since the gods are most likely to be found in the skies, all cultures have looked for meaning in the stars, as well as trying to explain where they came from. In Native North American mythology it was said that the Spider Grandmother span a web that was then covered in dew. She threw this into the heavens, thus creating the night sky.

The Greeks were keen watchers of the stars, and joined them together to form constellations. Each constellation was related to a mythological story: Ursa Major and Ursa Minor were the nymph Callisto and her son transformed into bears, for example, while the neighbouring constellation Draco represented the dragon killed by Jason (see p. 318). The ancient Egyptians, on the other hand, saw the same constellation as the hippo-headed god Tarawet. They believed that after death the soul would have to navigate the stars to reach heaven. The Aztec god associated with the night sky was Tezcatlipoca.

BELOW LEFT *This Aztec diagram relates stars to parts of the human body.* BELOW *The constellation Draco ('dragon') was said by the Greeks to commemorate the dragon killed by Jason.* OPPOSITE *An astronomer observes the star signs in this Armenian manuscript.*

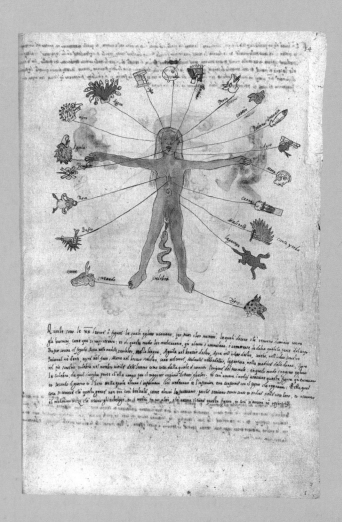

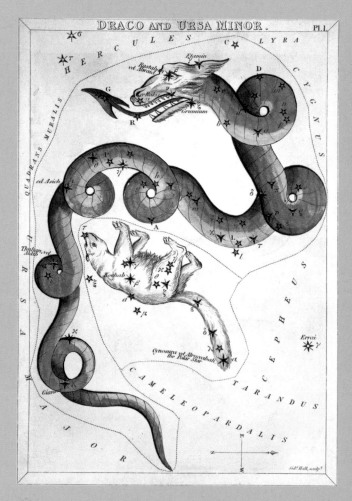

The Chinese identified four mythological beasts in the night skies: the Azure Dragon, the Black Tortoise, the Vermilion Bird and the White Tiger. These animals were also associated with the seasons, the cardinal points and the elements.

One North American Tlingit myth tells how all of the light in the world was hoarded by a single person. To get it back, the trickster Raven infiltrated the house disguised as a baby and was given a bag of stars to play with. He emptied the bag, and the stars floated up through the chimney into the sky.

BELOW *Byzantine diagram of the skies. Helios, in the centre, is conflated with Christ, while the apostles are aligned with the zodiac signs.*
RIGHT *Pottery tile of the Han dynasty showing animals that represent the major constellations and the cardinal points.* OPPOSITE *Aeon, the Roman god of time, turns a celestial sphere decorated with the signs of the zodiac. In front of him is the mother-earth goddess, Tellus (Gaia).*

The Gods in Love

Gods procreate in curious ways. The earliest Greek gods multiplied almost magically, while the later Olympians often adopted disguises in order to seduce others. In Aztec mythology the first god, Ometeotl ('Two God'), was both male and female. It gave birth to the four solar deities: Huitzilopochtli, Quetzalcoatl, Tezcatlipoca and Xipe Totec.

Zeus' infidelities were legendary: he had at least forty mortal and divine lovers, and fathered dozens of children, including Heracles, Aphrodite, Hermes, Dionysus and the Muses. He seduced humans in various forms – as a shower of golden coins (Danaë), a bull (Europa), an eagle (Ganymede), and even a cloud (Io). Odin inherited Zeus' fondness for women, despite his marriage to Frigg, whose name means 'beloved one'.

RIGHT *The god Wotan takes leave of the Valkyrie Brünnhilde, who in Richard Wagner's version of Norse myth was his daughter by the earth goddess Erda. Brünnhilde.* BELOW *Zeus appears to the unfortunate Semele, moments before she is incinerated by his glory.* OPPOSITE *Correggio's painting of Io seduced by Zeus in the form of a cloud.*

Other Olympian gods were not above infidelities. The beautiful Aphrodite was married to the lame blacksmith Hephaestus but had an affair with the god of war, Ares. Hephaestus fashioned a net to catch them in the act, and all of the gods came to watch the entrapped couple (as well as to appreciate the naked Aphrodite).

The archetypal faithful wife was Isis. In a story central to Egyptian mythology, Osiris was abducted by his brother Seth, who trapped him in a sarcophagus and threw him into a river. Isis scoured the world before she succeeded in finding her husband; although Seth had dismembered Osiris's body, Isis was able to reassemble him using magic and then to conceive Horus.

ABOVE *Aphrodite, Greek goddess of love, emerges from the sea in this carved relief.* OPPOSITE *The Hindu god Shiva bathes with his beloved Parvati.*

OPPOSITE *Hephaestus captures his wife, Aphrodite, with her lover, Ares.*
The other gods look on. ABOVE *The Hindu gods Vishnu and Lakshmi,*
his wife (both riding an elephant), meet Shiva, Parvati and Ganesha.

摩竭
饑竭

Weather Gods

For societies based on agriculture, weather is paramount. In ancient Greece the key weather god was Zeus: called the 'cloud-gatherer', he appears clutching lightning bolts, manufactured for him by three of the Cyclopes, a race of giants. Zeus shares similarities with the thunder gods Donar (German), Thor (Norse) and Taranis (Celtic).

In Yoruba mythology Shango was an earthly ruler who ascended to heaven to became a storm god. The Shinto storm god Susanoo, the brother of the sun deity Amaterasu, was banished to heaven after scaring his sister into a cave (see p. 42). The Aztec rain god Tlaloc was also associated with violent storms.

Ancient Babylon had a range of wind deities, including Tiamat and Marduk, as well as the demon Pazuzu, the south-west wind. In the *Enuma Elish* Marduk defeats Tiamat using the Four Winds. Later, in Canaan, we find the storm god Baal.

In Greek mythology the ruler of the winds was Aeolus. He gave Odysseus a bag containing all the winds to help him get home, but Odysseus' men opened it, causing a storm. Among the four winds was Zephyr, who in Botticelli's painting (see p. 62) is depicted blowing Venus to shore.

Japanese wind gods are also shown holding bags. The wind god Fujin let the winds out of his bag in order to clear away the mists that linger after creation. His brother was Raijin, the storm god. Meanwhile, in Aztec mythology Ehecatl – 'wind' – moved everything, including the sun, with his breath, although he himself had no permanent form.

OPPOSITE *One of these Japanese gods holds a wind bag, while the other holds a hammer for producing thunder.* ABOVE *The rain god Tlaloc exchanges cacao with the moon goddess.*

TOP *Scene from an Iron Age cauldron showing the Celtic thunder god Taranis grasping
a wheel.* ABOVE *Botticelli's beautiful Venus, born from a shell, is blown ashore by Zephyr.*
OPPOSITE *Thor rides in his goat-drawn chariot, his hammer crackling with thunderous energy.*

The Rainbow

Of all natural phenomena, the rainbow is among the most mysterious and magical. Past viewers must have taken it as the clearest sign possible that a supernatural realm existed.

On account of its form, the rainbow is often understood as a bridge. In Norse mythology, for example, it was called Bifröst and linked the world of humans with that of the gods; it had a dedicated guardian in the figure of Heimdallr. For the Greeks the rainbow was associated with the messenger goddess Iris.

The biblical tale of Noah describes the rainbow as a symbol of the covenant between God and humankind. A very similar story is found in the *Epic of Gilgamesh*, in which the great goddess Ishtar offers her rainbow necklace as a covenant that she will never forget the Great Flood.

ABOVE *In the Bible, the rainbow signals God's covenant with mankind after the Flood. Here, Noah prepares a thanksgiving sacrifice.*
OPPOSITE *Iris, the ancient Greek personification of the rainbow.*

In Hindu mythology, meanwhile, the rainbow is said to be the bow of Indra, the god of thunder and storms. It was also believed that the early kings of Tibet returned to heaven in the form of rainbows.

Some cultures associated the rainbow with snakes. A 'rainbow serpent' appears in both Aztec mythology and in Australian Aboriginal tradition, where it controls the waters.

OPPOSITE *Uldra, a Scandinavian spirit of the waterfall rainbow.* ABOVE *The Nordic gods cross the rainbow bridge, Bifröst.*

Messengers of the Gods

In the Abrahamic traditions, angels function as God's messengers, appearing to the devout in their hour of need, or making important announcements. For Christians, God's principal messenger is the archangel Gabriel, who appeared to Mary to announce that she was pregnant with Christ.

The main Classical messenger, alongside Iris, is Hermes (known to the Romans as Mercury). His winged sandals – made for him by Hephaestus – allowed him to fly between heaven and earth; and in his hand he held a snake-entwined wand called the *cadeceus*. One of Hermes' chief responsibilities was to guide the dead to the underworld.

ABOVE *Orpheus' severed head became an oracle – a link with the supernatural realm consulted by mortals.* OPPOSITE *Mercury appears in this fresco from Pompeii clutching his wand and wearing his winged sandals. Juno sits on a throne, with Iris behind her.*

Tricksters

||||||||||||||||||||||||||||||||||||||||||||||||||||||||||||||||

Tricksters endow myths with unpredictability, chaos and humour. Almost all are adept shape-shifters. Perhaps the best-known trickster is the Norse god Loki: the son of giants, he was instrumental in the death of Balder (see p. 162) and was punished by being chained to a rock, with a snake dripping venom onto his face. Loki's offspring include the giant wolf Fenrir, the Midgard Serpent and Hel.

The two key tricksters in Native American mythology are Coyote and Raven (see p. 224). Coyote was the first person to tell a lie, and introduced sickness and death into the world.

Yoruba culture has the trickster–messenger god Eshu (who, like Hermes, is the god of boundaries). On one occasion Eshu convinced the sun and moon to change places, throwing the universe into chaos. Meanwhile, the Ashanti culture in West Africa has the trickster spider Ananse, who created humankind.

The trickster Maui is a popular Polynesian deity, found everywhere from Hawaii to New Zealand. He used his grandmother's jawbone to slow down the sun and to fix the length of the day, and also gave mankind fire.

LEFT *This kneeling figure represents Eshu, a Yoruba god associated with trickery and surprise.* ABOVE RIGHT *The North American trickster Coyote in a canoe.* RIGHT *The birth of Maui, Polynesia's trickster god.* OPPOSITE *Loki's punishment was to be bound to a rock and to endure snake venom dripping onto his face.*

The Underworld

Perhaps because of their traditional burial practices, most mythologies see the area below the earth – the underworld – as the place of the dead.

The Greeks had two underworlds. The first was Hades, ruled over by the god of the same name, the brother of Zeus. Hades was not a place of punishment, but simply where the dead dwelt. Beneath Hades was Tartarus. In the *Iliad*, Zeus explains that Tartarus is 'as far beneath Hades as heaven is high above the earth'. It was a pit of suffering where the early chaos monsters – the Cyclopes and the Hecatonchaires, for instance – were put by Cronus, Zeus' father. Zeus let them out, and then put his father there instead. Typhon was confined to Tartarus, as was Tantalus (see p. 202).

Tartarus is not dissimilar to the Christian hell, the domain of Satan. The word 'hell' comes from the name of the Norse goddess of the underworld, Hel. In Mesopotamian mythology the underworld was ruled over by Ereshkigal, the sister of Ishtar, the Lady of Heaven. The two sisters were fiercely jealous of one another.

OPPOSITE *After failing in the attempt to overthrow Zeus, the Giants were consigned to the underworld.* BELOW *In Classical mythology Charon's boat ferried the dead across the Styx, the river that separated the dead from the living. The multi-headed dog Cerberus stood guard.*

T. Stothard. pinx.   London, Publish'd 1 Nov.r 1792. by Jeffryes & C.o Ludgate Hill.   F. Bartolozzi Sculp.t R.A.

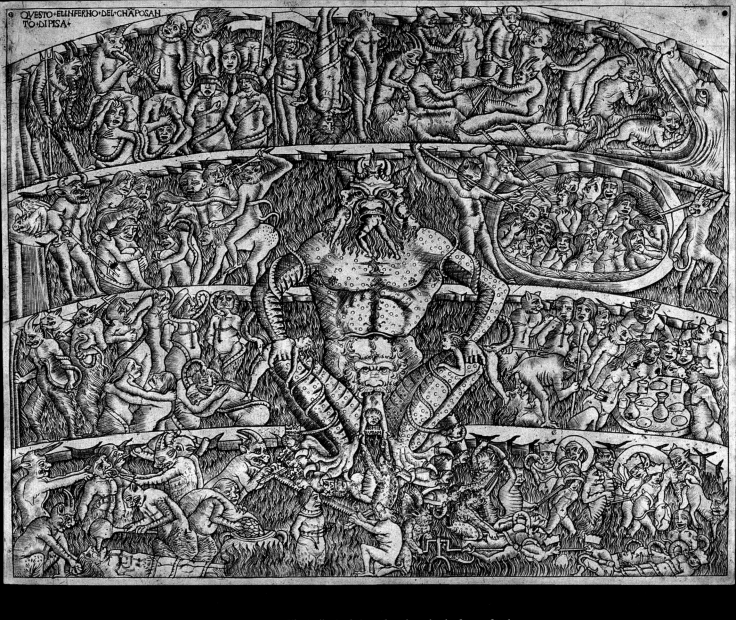

OPPOSITE ABOVE *The Valkyries being taken down by the forces of Hel during Ragnarok, the Norse doomsday.* OPPOSITE BELOW *The underworld is a place of shadows and strange creatures.* ABOVE *Satan oversees his hellish kingdom, surrounded by demons who torture the damned.*

OPPOSITE *Psyche descends to the underworld to collect water from the River Styx.* RIGHT *Hades, lord of the underworld, and his wife, Persephone.* BELOW *This 1st-century relief from Palmyra shows the Babylonian underworld god Nergal – here closely resembling Heracles – with the gods of the moon and the sun.*

ABOVE *The fearsome-looking Mesopotamian storm demon Pazuzu combines a lion's head, eagle's wings and scorpion's tail.* LEFT *A skeletal Aztec star demon, or tzitzimitl.* OPPOSITE *The Buddha meditates under the Boddhi tree, resisting the demons who tempt him.*

Demons

Demons play a variety of unpredictable roles in mythology, sometimes encouraging evil, sometimes punishing evil-doers.

In Hindu mythology demons are known as *asuras*, although they are not necessarily evil – in fact, some *asuras* are surprisingly devout. According to Vedic tradition, *asuras* and their heavenly counterparts, the *devas*, stem from the same creator. On occasion *asuras* fight the gods, but they also help them in the Churning of the Ocean of Milk (see p. 162). When the elixir of life appears, however, they try to steal it.

In the Judaeo-Christian religions, Satan began his career in heaven but was cast down to hell after rebelling against God. In later Christian tradition Satan became the personification of evil, the head of a hierarchy of demons, and above all a tempter.

Mesopotamian mythology has a range of storm demons, including the well-known Pazuzu. As in Hindu tradition, all gods and demons come from the same father, Anu. Fourteen demons were said to have helped the god Nergal reach the underworld, to visit Ereshkigal.

Demons are also to be found in Buddhism. Tibet, for example, has a tradition of spirits called *bDud*, which predate Buddhism but were incorporated into the pantheon. And Japanese folklore has the greatest number of demons, known collectively as *Oni*, as well as ghostly spirits called *Yokai*. *Oni* often appear in depictions of hell, wielding large iron clubs.

श्रीदेवी

श्रीदत्तात्रय

*Durga (far left),
an avatar of the
Hindu goddess Devi,
decapitates the buffalo
demon Shri Deri.*

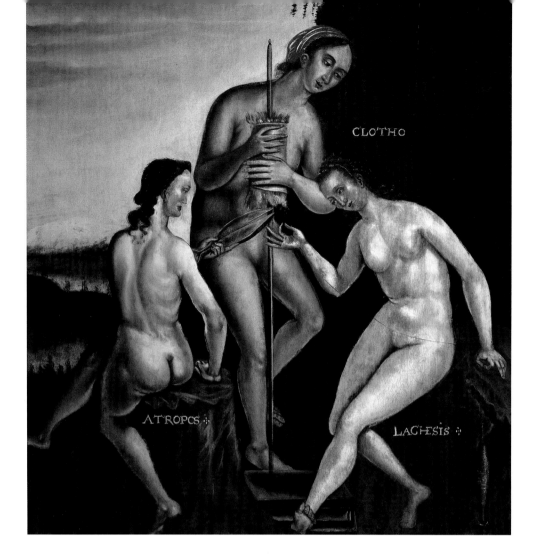

Other Supernatural Beings

Mythologies are full of peculiar supernatural creatures. Norse stories, for example, include the Ice Giants, who are occasional enemies of the Aesir (although at other times they marry them). Greek mythology provides the single-eyed giants called Cyclopes, as well as the Giants that attack Olympus.

Classical mythology offers perhaps the best range of supernatural beings who do not fit into the realm of the gods. Nymphs, for example, were nature spirits belonging to particular places: there were dryads, who were tree spirits (and connected especially to oak trees); the Hesperides, who tended a paradisiacal garden; and naiads, who guarded rivers, springs and streams. Other nymphs served particular gods, such as Pan.

Everybody feared the three Greek Fates (Moirae) – even the gods; they find their Norse equivalents in the Norns (see p. 192). Hindu mythology offers the snake-like beings called *nagas*. Their leader is Shesha, the snake upon whom Vishnu rests between bouts of creation (see p. 146).

ABOVE LEFT *The Three Greek Fates, called Clotho ('spinner'), Lachesis ('disposer of lots') and Atropos ('inevitable').* ABOVE *This house pole from British Columbia shows the cannibal ogress Dzonoqwa.* OPPOSITE *The Norse giant Baugi, accompanied by Odin, drills through a mountain to reach the mead of the poets.*

Hr̄ borar Baugi br̄ödur Suttungs Kvÿtbiorg
med Napinum Rata, eptir beidni Bölverks, er
Ödin var teyndur. So sem Seiger i Sextugustu
og fyrstu Dæmisögu Eddu.

Baugi

Rati

Kvÿtbiorg

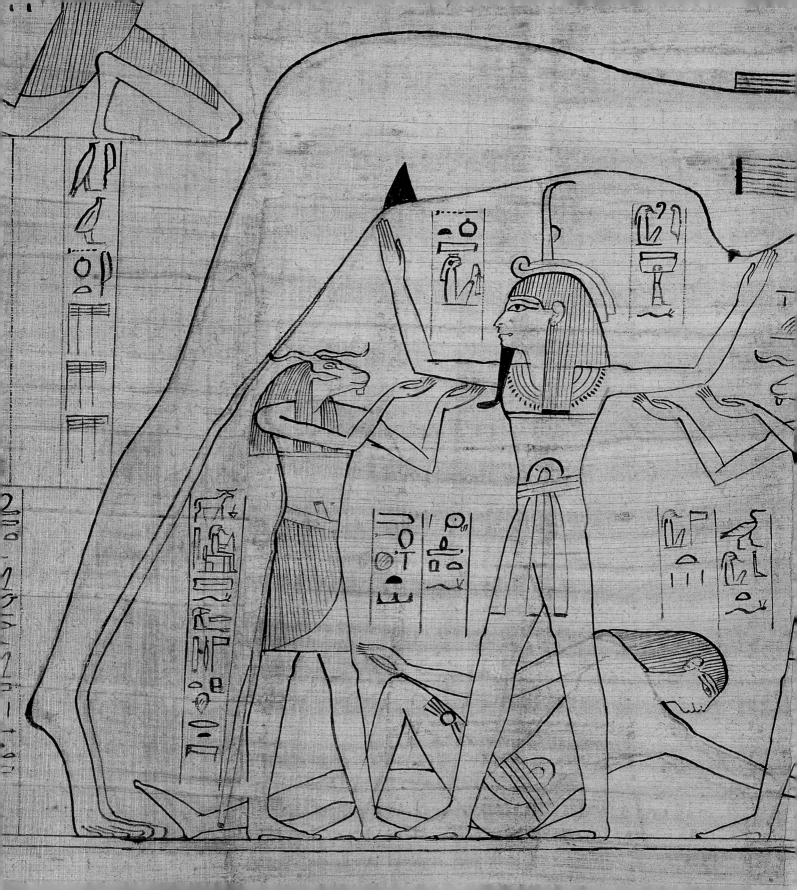

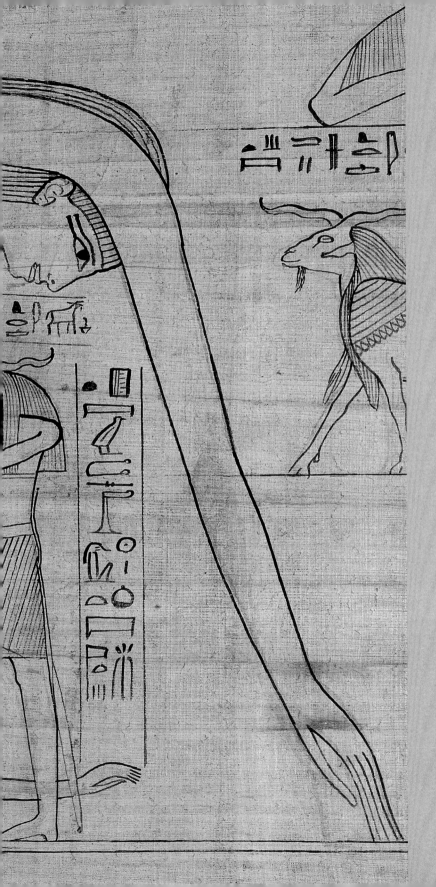

2

THE EARTH
||||||||||||||||||||||||||||||||||||||||||||

Just as mythologies attempt to explain human existence and the workings of the supernatural realm, they also concern themselves with our surroundings. Many of the earth's features – its mountains, rivers, ravines, waterfalls and deserts – evoke a sense of drama, and the landscape often is so beautiful and so treacherous that cultures around the world have inevitably sought meaning in it.

For the ancient Greeks, the earth was literally made up of gods. The first entity to emerge from primal chaos was Gaia, the embodiment of the earth. Gaia gave birth to the mountains and the sky (Uranus). Gaia and Uranus had offspring, including the Titans and the Cyclopes. Disgusted by his children, Uranus forced them back into Gaia – who, sick of her husband, gave the remaining son, Cronus, a sickle with which to castrate his father. Sky was separated from earth, allowing space for the rest of creation.

The figures of the Earth Mother and Sky Father are found in several mythologies, including Native American legends. In Nigeria the two are locked in a tight embrace that traps their children. Each child tries to prise them apart, but only one succeeds. In ancient Egyptian mythology Geb (earth) and Nut (sky) are separated by their father, Shu.

In Chinese legend the sky was raised by Pan Gu, who installed four pillars to keep it in place. After Pan Gu's death, his body became different parts of the landscape. This story of a 'dismembered god' is paralleled in ancient Mesopotamia, where Marduk split the corpse of Tiamat into two parts, the earth (her breasts, for example, became mountains) and the sky.

To this divine landscape were added various mythological episodes that might explain topographical curiosities. The myths of the Australian Aborigines are strongly connected to their immediate surroundings. Specific landmarks were formed by the Creator Beings during the period known as the Dreamtime: mountains could be fallen giants or iguanas, while other natural, geographical features are signs left by ancestors. Ravines and mountains are seen as carved out by giant thrashing snakes. The Aborigines' most sacred sites are natural features like Uluru (Ayers Rock).

Such local myths highlight an immediate link to the supernatural at the same time as providing tangible proof of a people's beliefs. Even today there are archaeologists trying to locate the site of Mount Ararat, where Noah's Ark supposedly came to rest after the Great Flood. These archaeologists' forebears in ancient Greece

PRECEDING PAGES *The Egyptian sky goddess Nut arcs over her brother-husband, the earth god Geb. Their father, Shu, separates them.* OPPOSITE *God, wearing a papal tiara, creates the land and seas, as related in the biblical Book of Genesis.* RIGHT *Noah oversees construction of the Ark, according to God's strict instructions.*

and Rome believed that the fossilized mammoth bones dug out of the ground were the remains of giants. The legend of a deluge that drowned the earth and nearly wiped out mankind is near universal. In Native American tales, the earth was brought to the surface, little by little, by 'earth-divers'. In Hindu mythology Vishnu's boar avatar, Varaha, retrieved the earth from the bottom of the seas.

Mythology gives us an insight into the worldviews of different cultures. Several traditions include the concept of the *axis mundi*, or the centre of the world. European maps from the medieval period placed Jerusalem at the centre, on account of its biblical importance. Others believed that the centre of the world was the Garden of Eden, source of the four rivers of Paradise. In Hindu mythology the centre of the universe is the mythical Mount Meru; for the Norse, it was Yggdrasil, the World Tree. Trees feature prominently in mythology, their growth, strength and longevity functioning as powerful metaphors.

Many cultures see the landscape as guarded by spirits. The Greeks had their naiads and dryads, who watched over forests and rivers, while in Norse mythology the same role was fulfilled by the protective *Landvættir*. In Japan, Korea and China, too, we find mountain gods and sprites, and the Celts believed in beings that guarded springs. South-East Asian mythology imbues rocks, plants and rivers with spirits: the Rice Spirit, for instance, plays an important role at harvest time.

Understandably, several myths reflect humanity's dependence on the rhythms of nature. In Egypt, the annual flooding of the Nile sustained the entire country, making the barren deserts fertile. In Mesopotamia, the shepherd king Dumuzi, consort of Ishtar, was forced to spend half of each year in the underworld – a story that accounted for the annual fertility cycle. Hittite and Hurrian mythology, meanwhile, had Telepinu, a god of farming and irrigation who was particularly popular in Anatolia. It was said that one day he became enraged and disappeared, taking all fertility with him, until one of his fellow gods managed to coax him back.

In Greek myth the same cycle is explained by the story of Persephone. This beautiful fertility goddess was the daughter of Demeter and Zeus. Unknown to Demeter, Zeus had promised Persephone to his brother Hades (Pluto), who duly carried her off to the underworld. Demeter searched everywhere for her daughter, neglecting her usual duties of tending to the earth. Eventually Zeus sent Hermes to retrieve Persephone, and Hades agreed to allow Persphone to spend two thirds of the year above ground. Her annual reemergence from the underworld provided the Greeks with an explanation for spring.

The Creation of the Earth

Precisely how the earth came into being is narrated in a variety of stories. Some cultures recognized the earth as female, being the counterpart of the male sky, and saw the separation of the two as vital for further creation. In the Judaeo-Christian tradition, God created the earth on the third day, having already separated the waters from the sky.

According to many world mythologies, the earth emerged from the waters. 'Earth-diver' legends can be found in Native American, Japanese, Sumatran and Indian traditions: a creature (often humble and unassuming, such as a turtle or a beetle) dives into the water to bring up earth, bit by bit, to create dry land.

In Chinese mythology Pan Gu separated sky and earth – *yin* and *yang* – with an axe. Growing to superhuman proportions, he then pushed the sky up further, after which he died, his body turning into the mountains, his breath becoming the wind, and his bones changing into mineral deposits.

BELOW *The artist John Martin captures the awe and drama of God's creation of the world.* OPPOSITE *In Chinese mythology Pan Gu created the world, separating heaven and earth.*

The *Axis Mundi*

In medieval Europe, maps of the known world, called *mappae mundi*, were often centred on Jerusalem, site of King Solomon's Temple and Christ's crucifixion. For Hindus and Buddhists, on the other hand, the universe centred on Mount Meru, or Sumeru (see p. 95), while in Norse tradition the world's centre was the trunk of Yggdrasil (see p. 118). Tartar mythology claimed a tree at the world's centre was directly connected with heaven.

For the Aztecs, the world's focus was their capital city of Tenochtitlan. Built on Lake Texcoco, Tenochtitlan was founded in about 1350 on the spot where an eagle was seen eating a snake on top of a large cactus – apparently a sign from the god Huitzilopochtli. At the city's heart was an extensive temple, with altars dedicated to Huitzilopochtli and Tlaloc.

ABOVE LEFT *The sight of an eagle perched on a cactus marked the location of the future Tenochtitlan. Waterways divided the city into four.* ABOVE RIGHT *This stone, called the* omphalos *('navel'), marked the centre of the Greek universe, at Delphi.* OPPOSITE *This* mappa mundi *places Jerusalem at the centre of the world. The Tower of Babel and Noah's Ark are also depicted.*

須弥

Mountains

As the parts of earth closest to the heavens, mountains have always had sacred significance. Their remoteness made them ideal dwelling places for gods: the Canaanite gods lived on Mount Saphon, near Ugarit, while the Greek gods lived on Mount Olympus.

Mount Meru in Hindu tradition was a mountain of staggering proportions (see pp. 40–41). Buddhism knows it as Sumeru, a giant peak in the form of an hourglass, scalable only by the pure of heart. Recreations of Sumeru can be found in the temple at Borobudur, in Java, and at Angkor Wat, Cambodia. Aztec temples are man-made peaks, just as Babylonian and Sumerian ziggurats are representations of holy mountains.

The Japanese regard mountains such as Mount Fuji as holy places, often off-limits to mortals. In Shinto legend, the home of the gods, Takamagahara, is to be found at the top of Mount Takachiho. The ancient spirit Sanshin is said to rule over all of the mountains of Korea, while Dangun, the country's legendary first king, thereafter became a mountain deity.

In the Judaeo-Christian tradition, Moses communed with god on Mount Sinai, receiving the Ten Commandments. The Gospels also relate how Christ was taken by Satan to a mountain top and offered all that he could see.

Mont St-Michel in northern France was a Celtic solar sanctuary before its monastery was established; King Arthur is supposed to have slain a giant there. The sacred mountain of Helgafel, in western Iceland, was not to be looked at without washing first, and living creatures were said to be immune from harm when on the mountain.

Some say that faith moves mountains, but in the Indian *Ramayana* epic the same feat is accomplished by the Hindu monkey god Hanuman. Sent to a mountain to fetch some herbs with which to treat the injured Lakshmana, he decides it would be quicker to bring back the entire mountain.

OPPOSITE *Hokusai's depiction of the hourglass-shaped Sumeru, home of the Buddhist gods.* ABOVE *The Japanese hero Tadatsune meets the goddess of Mount Fuji.*

OPPOSITE *Yama Uba, a wild mountain woman of Japanese folklore who dresses in leaves. The giant axe belongs to Kintaro.* ABOVE LEFT *The Greek giant Enceladus was punished for rebellion by being buried under Mount Etna. His fiery breath fuels the volcano.* ABOVE *The Hindu god Hanuman decides to take the entire mountain to Lakshmana. Here he holds the sun with his tail.*

Floods

||||||||||||||||||||||||||||||||||||||||||||||

Many Asian and Middle Eastern mythologies contain an account of a flood in which a disappointed god decides to wipe out humanity. The most famous example comes from the Bible: the pious Noah is told to build an ark to house examples of every species of animal. After the flood, Noah and his family repopulate the earth.

In the Mesopotamian *Epic of Gilgamesh*, Utnapishtim is advised by the god Enki to build an ark before Enki's brother, Enlil, sends a great deluge. Once the rains stop, Utnapishtim sends a bird – possibly a dove, as in the story of Noah – to find dry land, before disembarking and sacrificing to Enlil.

In Greek mythology Zeus, too, decides to flood the world. Prometheus, however, forewarns his son Deucalion to prepare a chest of provisions. Deucalion and his wife float around

in the chest for nine days. Once they are back on land, Zeus allows them to re-create mankind: they throw stones over their shoulders, and people appear. In Hindu myth, the human Manu is warned of the flood by Vishnu (in his fish form) and is able to save himself in time.

Tezcatlipoca ('smoking mirror') was one of the Aztec creator gods, along with Quetzalcoatl. While the earth was still entirely flooded, Tezcatlipoca fought with the earth monster Cipactli, which bit off his foot. Afterwards Cipactli was captured, killed and turned into the land.

OPPOSITE *Humanity is wiped out in the biblical Great Flood.*
ABOVE *The Aztec god Tezcatlipoca, who battled the earth monster Cipactli. Cipactli's body became the land.*

OPPOSITE *The Old Testament flood. Both animals and humans are doomed.* RIGHT *Noah's Ark here looks like little more than an elaborate chest.*

The Seas

The seas offer opportunities for trade and adventure, but are also full of mystery and danger – especially in the form of the strange creatures found there, such as the Bible's monstrous Leviathan, or the Midgard Serpent in Norse legend.

The seas and oceans are generally governed by gods. In Norse mythology the sea god is the giant Ægir, while in Greek stories the ruler of the seas was Poseidon, brother of Zeus and Hades. Poseidon married the sea nymph Amphitrite, and their offspring included the monster Charybdis (see p. 326) and the god Triton, who could calm the waves with his conch. When angered, Poseidon could provoke floods and earthquakes; horses and chariots were thrown into the sea to placate him. Aphrodite, too, was born from the sea, emerging from the castrated genitals of Uranus.

There is a Japanese sea spirit called Watatsumi. One day the fisherman Hoori lost his brother's fishing hook, so descended to Watatsumi's red-and-white coral palace to retrieve it. There he met – and subsequently married – the sea god's daughter, Otohime. They went on to become the grandparents of Japan's first emperor. Watatsumi is sometimes conflated with the sea dragon Ryujin. Another story relates how a second fisherman, Urashima Tar, visited Ryujin's palace for three days; when he returned to his village, he discovered he was 300 years in the future.

BELOW *Nereus, known to ancient Greeks as 'the Old Man of the Sea', rides a hippocamp, trident in hand.* OPPOSITE *Poseidon and Amphitrite ride in a quadriga in this 4th-century mosaic from Cirta (in modern Algeria).*

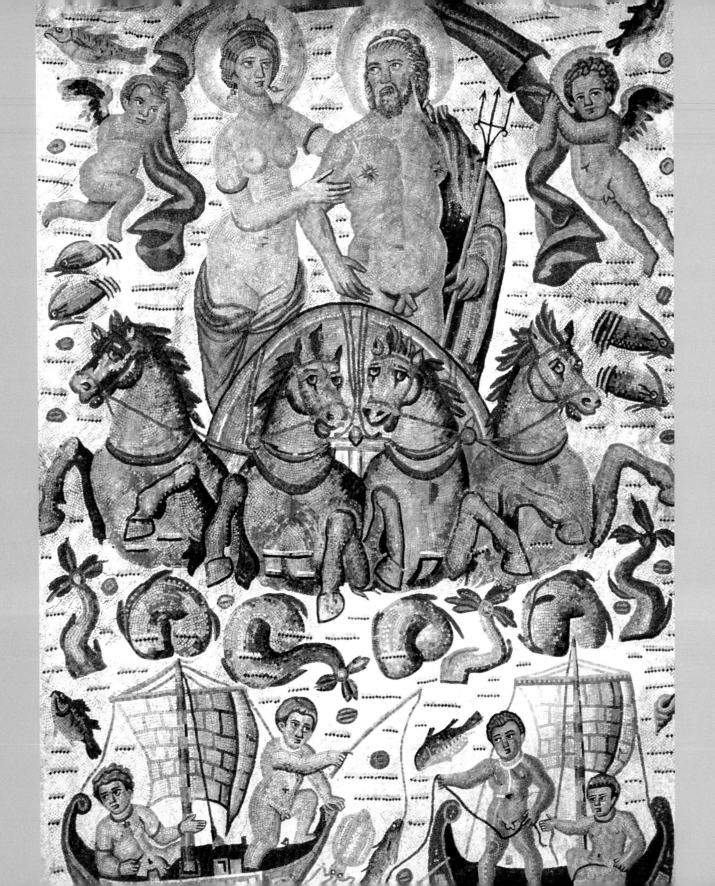

ABOVE LEFT *Triton blows his conch shell to pacify the sea.* ABOVE *The Classical goddess Aphrodite (Venus) was born from the sea, springing from the surf.* OPPOSITE *William Blake depicts Leviathan (bottom) as a fearsome sea serpent. Above is Behemoth, his counterpart on land.*

LEFT *The Japanese princess Tamatori being pursued by Ryujin, having stolen a pearl.* OPPOSITE *The Hindu god Varuna, lord of the oceans.*

వరుణమంతు
ৰ্তুత్ట 115

Dieu de l'eau

Rivers

Rivers have special local significance around the world, in part as sources of fresh water. It was two rivers, the Tigris and the Euphrates, that defined the Mesopotamian cultures, while the Nile was central to Egyptian civilization, its annual flooding being vital to agriculture. The Egyptian god Hapy, who was responsible for the annual flooding, is often shown binding together the kingdoms of Upper and Lower Egypt, just as the Nile does.

In India the most important river is the Ganges, which is personified in Hinduism as the goddess Ganga. Ganga fell to earth (landing on Shiva's head) to help humanity cleanse their sins. Another Hindu river deity, Saraswati, was the consort of Brahma.

In the Bible, the four rivers of Paradise – the Euphrates, Tigris, Pishon and Gihon – flow from Eden. And in Greek mythology, the River Acheron divides the living from the dead. Other important rivers coming from the underworld included the Styx ('Hate'), Phlegethon ('Sorrow') and Cocytus ('Lamentation'). Gods swore oaths on the Styx, and Achilles was dipped in it as a baby to make him invincible. In Japanese Buddhist tradition, the dead must cross the River Sanzu – the good via a bridge, and the bad through the dragon-filled waters.

OPPOSITE *Hapy is the Egyptian god of the flooding Nile. Here he binds together Upper and Lower Egypt, just like the Nile.* RIGHT *Ganga, goddess of the Ganges, descends from heaven onto Shiva's head.*

Springs

In Celtic mythology springs were the homes of goddesses: Sulis, to give one example, was a local deity connected with the place known by the Romans as Aquae Sulis (modern-day Bath, in south-west England). In Germanic mythology springs were associated with Wotan (Odin), and in the 11th century Adam of Bremen described how human sacrifices were drowned in a sacred spring at the temple at Uppsala, in modern-day Sweden.

The Well of Urd watered the Norse World Tree, Yggdrasil, guarded by the three Norns (see p. 192). The water of this well was so holy that it turned anything that touched it white (such as swans, who were said to drink there).

In ancient Greece each spring had its own nymph. The most famous was the Pierian Spring, in Macedonia, which was sacred to the Muses, and the source of creativity and knowledge. Those consulting the Oracle of Delphi first purified themselves in the Castalian Spring – a source that was guarded by the monster Python until Apollo killed it.

In the Bible, one of Moses' miracles, as he led the Israelites out of Egypt and to the Promised Land, was to strike his staff against a rock and cause water to gush out. In later Christian iconography, fountains are associated with life and salvation.

BELOW *Fountains and springs are associated with nymphs in Classical mythology.* OPPOSITE ABOVE *Coventina – here shown in triple form – was a Romano-British goddess of springs and wells. This relief is from a well in northern England.* OPPOSITE BELOW *An artist's impression of the pagan temple at Uppsala, complete with sacrificial well.*

ONTIS NYMPHA SACRI SOM
VM NE RVMPE QVIESCO ·

NAVE NAVE MOE

OPPOSITE ABOVE *This image of Apollo and the Muses on Mount Parnassus includes the Castalian Spring, fount of inspiration.* OPPOSITE BELOW *Moses strikes a rock with his staff, and water pours forth, saving the Israelites.* ABOVE *Paul Gauguin captures the mystery of a sacred spring in Polynesia.*

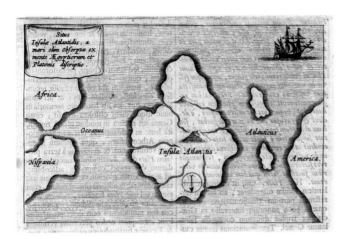

Islands

||||||||||||||||||||||||||||||||||||||||||||||||

The Greek gods Apollo and Artemis were born on the island of Delos, in the Aegean Sea. Yet it was no ordinary island: Hera, discovering that Leto was pregnant by her husband, Zeus, forbade her to give birth on land or water. However, the island of Delos, which was believed to be floating, offered an ideal solution. According to Homer, Aeolus, god of the winds, lived on another floating island, called Aeolia.

In Arthurian legend, the island of Avalon was where the sword Excalibur was forged. The home of the enchantress Morgana le Fay, it was a magical island, famous for its beautiful apples. Some legends tell that King Arthur was taken there to die.

Some islands are paradises on earth. In Chinese mythology Penglai Island is the home of the Eight Immortals. In Irish Celtic legends Tír na nÓg was the island of youth, free from sickness and death. One legend tells how the poet Oisín visited for a year, but when he returned to Ireland he discovered that 300 years had passed.

The Maori names for the North and South Islands of New Zealand are Te Ika-a-Maui and Te Waka-a-Maui: 'the fish of Maui' and 'the canoe of Maui'. The Polynesian trickster was said to have stood on the latter as he fished up the former.

The best-known mythical island, however, is probably the fabled Atlantis. According to Plato, the island's inhabitants had attempted to invade Athens in about 9600 BC, but had failed, and afterwards the island sank.

OPPOSITE *The trickster Maui was said to have fished up the North Island of New Zealand.* ABOVE *Athanasius Kircher's impression of Atlantis, situated in the middle of the Atlantic.* RIGHT *The mythical Penglai Island, home of the Eight Immortals in Chinese mythology.*

Trees

||||||||||||||||||||||||||||||||||||

The greatest of all mythical trees was Yggdrasil, the giant ash that in Norse mythology supported the universe. Its roots were constantly being nibbled by snakes, while an eagle guarded its peak. Trees played an important role in Germanic mythology: a giant, magical tree at the temple at Uppsala remained green year-round, while Germanic tribes used sacred groves for sacrifice, much as the Celts did.

Sacred groves are found around the world. The ancient rites associated with a grove in Ariccia, near Rome, inspired James Frazer's *The Golden Bough*, and oak groves were particularly associated with the Roman goddess of the hunt, Diana. Oaks were also sacred to Druids. In Nigeria the Osun-Osogbo sacred grove is dedicated to the fertility goddess Osun.

In Christianity, Adam's fall from grace began when he ate the forbidden fruit of the Tree of Knowledge; some apocryphal legends claim that Christ's cross was made from its wood.

The Tree of Life, meanwhile, appears in Mesopotamian art, tended by priests, gods or kings. Taoist myths tell of peach trees that provide immortality, just as Idunn's golden apples in Germanic mythology provide eternal life.

The founder of Buddhism, Siddhartha Gautama, was born under a sal tree, as his mother clung to one of its branches. Later he received enlightenment under a sacred fig tree, now known as the Bodhi tree.

According to one legend, the handsome Adonis, with whom Aphrodite fell in love, was born from a tree – his mother, Myrrha, had been turned into one. And according to some Egyptian myths, Isis and Osiris too had been born from a tree, this time an acacia.

ABOVE *Dryads are Classical tree spirits, particularly associated with oak trees.* OPPOSITE *The Greek nymph Daphne is turned into a laurel tree as the lovestruck Apollo pursues her.*

LEFT *A Japanese tree spirit.* ABOVE *The Norse World Tree, Yggdrasil, and the animals that live in it.* OPPOSITE *The Virgin Mary and Eve feed a crowd from a curious tree, symbolizing salvation on the left, death on the right.*

3

HUMANKIND
||||||||||||||||||||||||||||||||||||||||||||

Being self-aware, humans want to explain themselves, to fit themselves into a narrative. Where do we come from? Who created us, why and how? Although we humans like to believe that we have some sort of purpose, myths often downplay humanity's role: in Mesopotamian mythology, the gods created man to do their work digging irrigation canals. According to the Bible and the Maya text *Popol Vuh*, we were created in order to praise the creator.

How were we made? The ancient Egyptians believed the ram-headed god Khnum fashioned humans out of clay. Australian Aboriginal myth maintains that man was released from clay: we already existed, and the early creators simply cut us out of the primordial slime.

Other traditions sometimes relate how humanity has emerged in stages. For the Aztecs, we evolved from a lower to a higher form, in a sequence of five ages equated with the Five Suns. Greek mythology, however, reverses the order, cataloguing man's descent from the splendid Age of Gold (under the rule of Cronus) to the Age of Iron, in which humans live in misery.

On other occasions humankind appears in an instant, ready formed. In South American Chibcha myth, the first woman emerged from a lake and gave birth to a son, with whom she then procreated (most mythologies tolerate incest, at least in the early stages of creation). The biblical Adam is created at God's command, and made in the creator's own image; in other traditions most gods take on human form, insignificant as humanity is.

Eve, however, was created from one of Adam's ribs. In many myths man was created before woman (thus establishing, or attempting to justify, a hierarchy), and women hold an ambiguous place in mythology, reflecting their roles in contemporary society. The Greek Pandora is sent by the gods to stir up trouble among men. In the Maya *Popol Vuh*, the gods Gucumatz and Tepeu, fearing that their male creations were too perfect, decide to cloud their judgment by creating women. Yet, as the *Popol Vuh* makes clear, both sexes are essential for reproduction. The differences between the sexes are emphasized in the enlarged genitalia of Greek Herms and Celtic Sheela-na-gigs.

PRECEDING PAGES
*Adam and Eve –
according to the
Bible, the first man
and the first woman
– in the Garden
of Eden.* OPPOSITE
*During mankind's
Silver Age, life was
agricultural and
pastoral.* RIGHT
*God creates man
beneath the freshly
made moon and
stars.*

Many mythologies focus on the bond between brothers and sisters. Gods tend to fit into neat family trees that humans might relate to, often sharing the petty squabbles and jealousies found in human families. In the mortal realm, the biblical story of Cain and Abel is an archetypal tale of warring brothers, in which one kills the other for being God's favourite. In Roman legend Romulus argues with his twin, Remus, and kills him.

Twins hold a particular fascination; one is often good, and the other bad. The Yoruba of Nigeria value twins highly (they have the world's highest birth rate of twins), and they have a dedicated deity, called Orisha Ibeji. If one of a pair of twins dies, they are represented by a sculpture, to restore the balance.

In the Bible, St Paul's First Letter to the Corinthians describes the human body as a temple. Different parts of the body certainly have their own symbolism: eyes, for example, stood for gods in ancient Egypt, while the heart was seen as the home of the soul. Curiously, during the Egyptian mummification process that would prepare the dead for the afterlife, the brains were discarded as worthless, while the heart was left in the body. Hair, too, appears in myths, sometimes related to strength, as with the biblical Samson.

Myths attempt to explain human behaviour. The inner workings of our minds remain even today a great mystery to us. Many myths are concerned with the strange process of sleep, and dreams have always been a source of revelation. Dreams, such as that experienced by Joseph in the Old Testament, or Jacob's vision of the ladder of angels, connect humans to the supernatural realm.

The Sphinx asked Oedipus a timeless riddle: what walks on four legs in the morning, two legs in the afternoon, and three legs in the evening? The answer was man, who crawled, walked and then hobbled on a stick. Ageing heralds the coming of death, the greatest mystery of all. Death is not necessarily final in mythology, being often only symbolic, and followed by rebirth or the awakening of new life.

Self-sacrifice – the death of one for the good of many – is a common moralizing theme in mythology, found in Christianity and in Aztec and Norse mythology, where Odin hangs himself. Other figures, such as Castor and Pollux, choose to die (or half die) in the place of another. Yet even after death there is the promise of resurrection: even after the decisive final battle of Ragnarok, in which all die, at least some of the Norse gods will be reborn, led by the good god Balder.

LEFT *Ishtar, the Mesopotamian fertility goddess, surrounded by creatures of the sea and air.* OPPOSITE *The Last Judgment of humankind, as depicted in a 15th-century manuscript.*

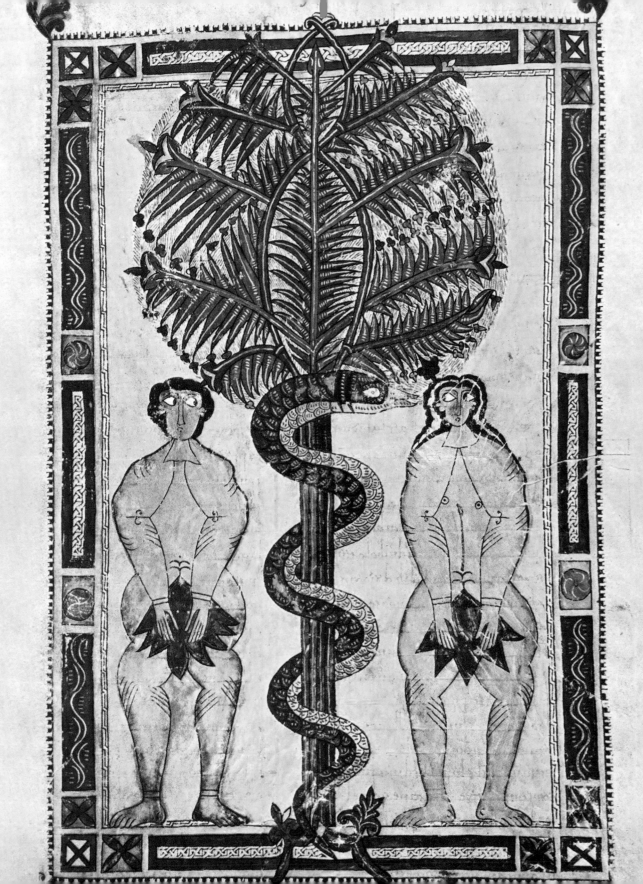

The Creation
of Man

In Polynesian mythology the first man, Tiki, was fashioned from red ochre. The Maya *Popol Vuh* text describes how the god-magicians Gucumatz and Tepeu tried fashioning humans from mud and clay before settling on maize. In some Greek traditions Prometheus modelled humanity out of water and clay; and the second creation story contained in the biblical Book of Genesis describes how 'the Lord God formed man of the dust of the ground, and breathed into his nostrils the breath of life; and man became a living soul'.

One Greek tradition maintains that Zeus created humans in a Golden Age, when they did not have to work – a situation similar to that in the Garden of Eden. This was followed by the Silver and Bronze Ages (not to be confused with the historical Bronze Age), before the Heroes arrived. The final period is the Age of Iron, in which we live today. Nothing is perfect, and we are beset by war and strife, toil and labour. After the flood (see p. 99), Deucalion and his wife Pyrrha repopulated the world by tossing stones over their shoulders: his became men, and hers became women.

Mythology also attempts to account for humankind's great variety. In Japanese tradition the first couple were called Izanagi and Izanami. They dipped a spear into the primordial brine, and a drop falling from the spear formed the first island, where they lived. Their first child was deformed, because in the wedding ceremony the woman, Izanami, had spoken first. The second time, Izanagi was the first to speak, and thereafter they had many healthy children. The Mesopotamian creator goddess, Nammu, was challenged by the (drunken) mother goddess Ninmah, who claimed that she, too, could create humans. Although each of her creations was disabled – some blind, some lame – Enki found them roles in society.

OPPOSITE *After eating the forbidden fruit, Adam and Eve were ashamed of their nakedness.* RIGHT *Izanagi and Izanami – Japan's first man and woman – create islands using a heavenly spear.*

REPARATIO GENERIS HVMANI

OPPOSITE *The Norse figures of Líf and Lífthrasir alone will survive the doomsday scenario of Ragnarok, and then repopulate the earth.* TOP *Deucalion and his wife, Pyrrha, throw stones that turn into people.* ABOVE *Some myths describe Prometheus as the creator of man. Here he animates his creations with fire.*

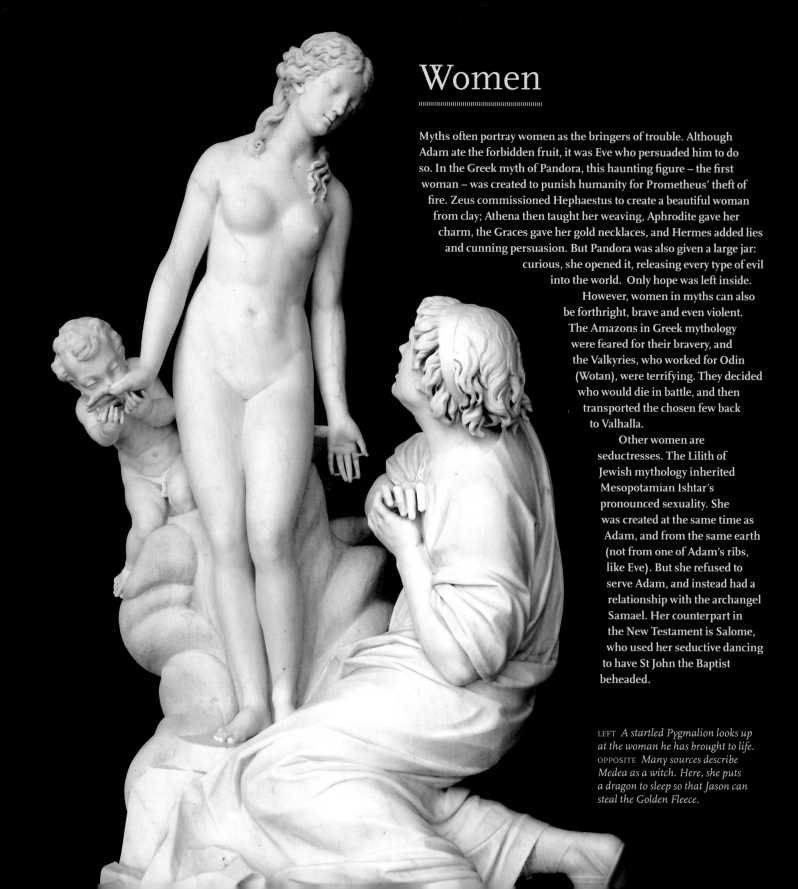

Women

Myths often portray women as the bringers of trouble. Although Adam ate the forbidden fruit, it was Eve who persuaded him to do so. In the Greek myth of Pandora, this haunting figure – the first woman – was created to punish humanity for Prometheus' theft of fire. Zeus commissioned Hephaestus to create a beautiful woman from clay; Athena then taught her weaving, Aphrodite gave her charm, the Graces gave her gold necklaces, and Hermes added lies and cunning persuasion. But Pandora was also given a large jar: curious, she opened it, releasing every type of evil into the world. Only hope was left inside.

However, women in myths can also be forthright, brave and even violent. The Amazons in Greek mythology were feared for their bravery, and the Valkyries, who worked for Odin (Wotan), were terrifying. They decided who would die in battle, and then transported the chosen few back to Valhalla.

Other women are seductresses. The Lilith of Jewish mythology inherited Mesopotamian Ishtar's pronounced sexuality. She was created at the same time as Adam, and from the same earth (not from one of Adam's ribs, like Eve). But she refused to serve Adam, and instead had a relationship with the archangel Samael. Her counterpart in the New Testament is Salome, who used her seductive dancing to have St John the Baptist beheaded.

LEFT *A startled Pygmalion looks up at the woman he has brought to life.*
OPPOSITE *Many sources describe Medea as a witch. Here, she puts a dragon to sleep so that Jason can steal the Golden Fleece.*

EVA PRIMA PANDORA

ABOVE *This intriguing painting combines the myths of Eve and Pandora into a single figure.* OPPOSITE *Pygmalion watches, enraptured, as his sculpture comes to life.*

Twins

Romulus and Remus, the two figures in Rome's foundation myth, were said to be descended from Aeneas on their mother's side, their father being either Hercules (Heracles) or Mars. As adults, they argued over where Rome should be founded, and in the ensuing fight Remus was killed.

Sometimes twins were polarized. According to several Zoroastrian stories, Ahura Mazda and Angra Mainyu had been born of the same mother, but while the first embodied good and wisdom, the second embodied evil. This fundamental duality informs all of Zoroastrianism. In Aztec mythology Xolotl was the twin of Quetzalcoatl, but stood for death, whereas his twin stood for life; he was the evening star to Quetzalcoatl's morning star.

In the Maya *Popol Vuh*, among the central characters are the Hero Twins Hunahpu and Ixbalanque. Both monster-slayers, they descended into the underworld, where they defeated the rulers there in a ball game. They later became the sun and moon.

In Classical mythology we find the celebrated twins Castor and Pollux. Known as the Dioscuri, they shared a mother but had different fathers, meaning that Castor was mortal and Pollux immortal. When Castor died, Pollux gave up half of his immortality to save him. They were transformed into the constellation Gemini ('twins'). Similarly, although Heracles' father was Zeus, his twin, Iphicles, was fathered by the mortal Amphitryon.

OPPOSITE *The Maya Hero Twins descended into the underworld, where they met the Lords of Xibalba, one of whom is shown here.* RIGHT *The famous sculpture of Romulus and Remus being suckled by a she-wolf.*

137

RIGHT *Twins have great importance in Yoruba culture and mythology, and are often portrayed in sculpture.* OPPOSITE *Castor and Pollux were famous twins of Classical mythology and emblems of self-denial.*

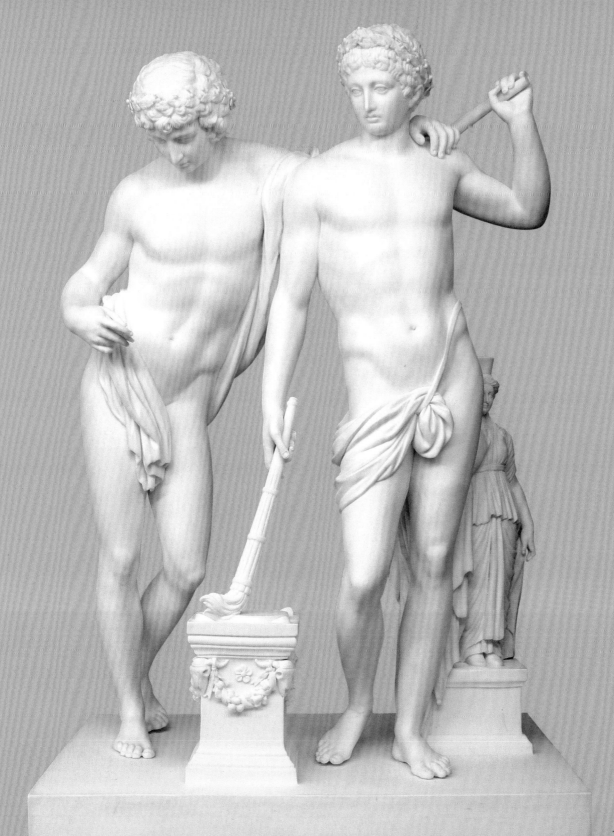

Sexuality

The doctrine of 'original sin' – a direct result of Adam and Eve's disobedience to God in the Garden of Eden – has always been closely connected with sex, and Christians believe that the chain was broken only by the Virgin Mary. In Greece the virgin goddess was Artemis, whose attendants swore a vow of chastity. After Callisto, one of her followers, was seduced by Zeus, it was Callisto whom Artemis punished.

Many myths delight in gods cross-dressing. In Norse mythology Thor dresses as a bride to infiltrate the Giants' palace and retrieve his hammer. And after accidentally killing the hero Iphitus, Heracles is obliged to serve Queen Omphale, dressing as a woman. Homosexuality also appears in mythology: one of the best-known stories concerns Zeus' seduction of the beautiful boy Ganymede; and the unfortunate Orpheus was murdered by women for 'inventing' homosexuality.

Perhaps the most famous myth involving sexuality is that of Oedipus. Warned by the Delphic Oracle that he would kill his father and marry his mother, Oedipus was distraught. When he discovered that the prophecy had been fulfilled, he put out his eyes, and his mother hanged herself.

BELOW *It was said that Orpheus died at the hands of Thracian women, furious that he had converted their husbands to homosexuality.* OPPOSITE ABOVE *The beautiful boy Ganymede was carried off by Zeus – in eagle form – to be the gods' cup-bearer.* OPPOSITE BELOW *Zeus seduces the beautiful Callisto by disguising himself as Artemis.*

BAR · SPRANGERS · ANT · FES17 ·

OPPOSITE *People enjoyed hearing of the great heroes and gods of mythology dressed as women. Here it is Thor's turn.* RIGHT *Heracles spins wool for Omphale. She is wearing his lionskin and wielding his club.*

Sleep and Dreams

For the Greeks, the god Morpheus was the shaper of dreams. He was the son of either Nyx (night) or Hypnos (Sleep), and one of the Oneiroi – three spirits who brought dreams to those who slept. Morpheus was responsible for the dreams of kings and rulers. The myth of Endymion, meanwhile, tells of a handsome shepherd boy put into an everlasting sleep by the moon goddess Selene, so that she could gaze upon him every night.

In the Old Testament, perhaps the best-known dreamer is Joseph. Sold into slavery by his brothers, he later became an adviser to Pharaoh in Egypt; his dreams warned of impending famine, allowing the Egyptians to stockpile their food.

The Hindu god Vishnu sleeps between bouts of creation. He is typically depicted on the back of the many-headed snake Shesha, his feet being massaged by his wife.

BELOW *Joseph tells his family about two of his prophetic dreams; they remain uninterested.* OPPOSITE *The moon goddess Selene gazes upon the enchanted Endymion.*

OPPOSITE *Vishnu reclines on the serpent Shesha. On the lotus that stems from Vishnu's navel sits Brahma.* RIGHT *In the Old Testament, Jacob dreams of a ladder of angels that extends to heaven.*

The Eye

The ancient Egyptians used the eye as a protective symbol, referring to it as the 'Eye of Horus', the 'Eye of Ra', or as the *wedjat*. Some myths claimed that Seth, in the form of a wild boar, had torn out Horus' left eye, the moon. Nights fell into complete darkness, but Thoth searched for and recovered the eye, restoring it to the heavens.

Odin sacrificed an eye to drink from the fountain of wisdom, and the single-eyed Cyclops Polyphemus was blinded by Odysseus. In the Bible, Jacob fools his blind father into making him his main heir, by putting on a coat that mimicked his brother Esau's hairy skin. And among his many miracles, Jesus healed several blind men.

Eyes can also be a source of power. The concept of the cursing 'evil eye' can be found around the world, and its malevolence warded off with amulets. The god Shiva is often depicted with an extra, vertical, eye in his forehead. Though it mainly looks inwards, he also uses it to burn away desire.

ABOVE *Christ's miracles included healing the blind.* BELOW *This 18th-century Rajasthani manuscript shows the 'third eye' – one of the traditional centres of spiritual power in Hinduism.* OPPOSITE *An Egyptian craftsman kneels below a* wedjat *eye.*

The Heart

The role of the heart in human anatomy was for a long time misunderstood. Neverthless, the Egyptians saw it as perhaps the most important of the body's organs, and it was left inside the deceased during mummification. It was believed that, once an individual was in the underworld, their heart would be weighed against the feather of Ma'at to determine whether they had led a good life worthy of reward.

In some branches of Christianity the Sacred Heart of Jesus became a popular symbol. Arising out of mystical visions, it symbolizes purity, sacrifice and Christ's love for mankind. Similarly, his mother, Mary, is said to have an Immaculate Heart.

OPPOSITE *The weighing of the heart of the scribe Ani by the jackal-headed god Anubis, from the Book of the Dead.* ABOVE *A Chinese diagram of the heart, above two medicinal symbols.* ABOVE RIGHT *Souls in purgatory look up to the five wounds received by Christ during his crucifixion. They are flanked by two images of his Sacred Heart.*

Self-Sacrifice

Self-sacrifice is a common theme among gods and heroes, who put the good of society, or access to knowledge, above their own lives. A good example is Prometheus, who gave humanity the gift of fire knowing that he would invoke Zeus' wrath. His punishment was to have his liver pecked out by an eagle every day (and every day it would grow anew).

In Aztec mythology life was possible only because of Nanahuatzin's act of self-sacrifice. After the extinction of the Fourth Sun, this humble god burned himself on a pyre to become the Fifth Sun, Tonatiuh, who thereafter demanded constant human sacrifice. Another deity, Xipe Totec, flayed himself in order to feed humanity. For this reason he was presented with offerings of flayed human skins, and is often shown wearing a flayed skin himself.

Scapegoats expiate the sin of an entire people – as did Jesus Christ. His crucifixion by the Romans was a blood sacrifice, paying for Adam and Eve's original sin. Just as his birth had been humble, his death was humiliating. The cycle of events surrounding Christ's death became central to Christianity, and the instruments of his torture are mainstays of Christian iconography.

The Norse god Odin also sacrificed himself. According to the *Poetic Edda*, he hung himself on a 'windy tree', often taken to mean Yggdrasil (see p. 118), in order to learn the truth of the runes from Mimir's head, located at its roots. According to the *Havamal* text, Odin was also speared, echoing the lancing of Christ on the cross. A 10th-century runestone from Jelling, in Denmark, shows Christ crucified on a tree – perhaps conflating the two traditions.

ABOVE LEFT *A jade mask of Xipe Totec, the 'flayed god'.* ABOVE *A runestone in Jelling, Denmark, appears to merge Christ's sacrifice with that of Odin.* OPPOSITE *Prometheus is bound to a rock, his liver pecked out daily by an eagle.*

Cornelis cort fe. Titianus 1566

ABOVE *Christ's sacrifice on the cross – greatly emphasized in the Isenheim Altarpiece – is central to Christianity.* OPPOSITE *This votive work commemorates the instruments of Christ's torture and death.*

Death

Mythologies, always thinking beyond everyday life, largely refuse to accept that death is the end. The Egyptians routinely mummified society's more important members, according to the instructions of Anubis. The deceased were buried with things they might need in the next life, including models of servants. Spells in the Book of the Dead helped the deceased pass through the underworld to the afterlife. After having their hearts weighed (see p. 150), the righteous progressed to a place of rest called Aaru. Inca burials also included items for the next life.

The spirits of ancestors were often thought to be powerful – as is the case in China and Japan – and it was vital to appease them. The Greek god of death was

OPPOSITE *This Egyptian papyrus shows the dead drinking the waters in Duat.* ABOVE *Valkyries collected the souls of the heroic dead, to transport them to Valhalla.* RIGHT *The shrouded, silent dead are ferried across the River Styx by Charon.*

Thanatos, the brother of Hypnos (Sleep). Hermes led the dead to the underworld, where they crossed the River Styx on Charon's ferry; indeed, the dead were always buried with a coin to pay for the journey. After passing the three-headed hound Cerberus, they reached a crossroads from which they went to the paradise-like Elysian Fields, the hellish Tartarus (see p. 73), or the Asphodel Meadows (similar to the Catholic purgatory, a place for the cleansing of sins).

In Norse mythology the bravest warriors would be plucked from the battlefield by the Valkyries (see p. 132). They would be taken to Valhalla, Odin's hall in Asgard, to eat, drink and wait for Ragnarok, when they would fight the giant wolf Fenrir.

BELOW *Hypnos and Thanatos gather the body of a slain hero from the battlefield.* OPPOSITE *The eternally fearless Heracles confronts the figure of Death.*

ABOVE *The trial of a dead soul in the court of Yama, the Hindu and Buddhist god of the underworld.* OPPOSITE *The death of the Buddha.*

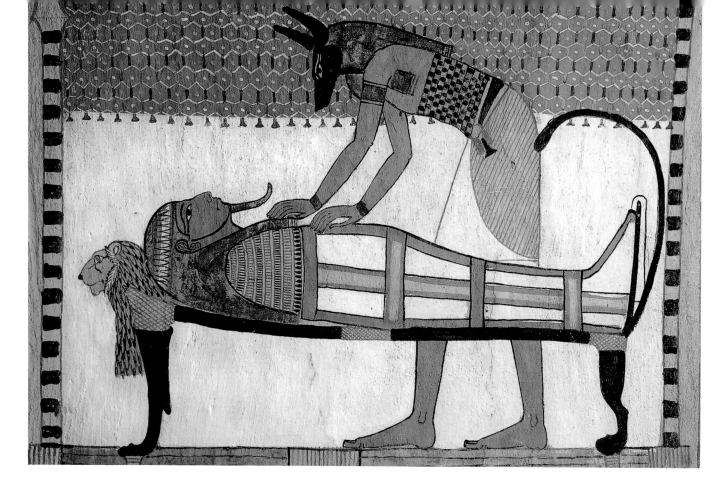

Eternal Life and Resurrection

Immortality tends to be the prerogative of the gods, but even they sometimes have to work for it. The Hindu gods, fearing that they were losing their immortality, decided to create more *amrita*, the nectar of everlasting life. To do this, they were obliged to churn the Ocean of Milk, which they did using a snake wrapped around Mount Meru balanced on a turtle (an avatar of Vishnu). One end of the serpent was pulled by the demons, the other end by the gods. When the *amrita* was produced, the demons and gods fought over it; happily, the gods were victorious.

In Norse and Germanic myth cycles, the gods' youth comes from the golden apples tended by the goddess Idunn. The Greek gods ate ambrosia, which gave them ageless immortality, while Medea, wife of the hero Jason, convinced the daughters of King Pelias that by murdering and boiling the king he might recover his youth. Pelias did not survive, and Jason and Medea were exiled.

The best-known tale of resurrection is that of Christ related in the New Testament. According to apocryphal accounts, in the three days following his crucifixion Christ descended into hell, where he rescued the souls of the dead.

The Norse story of Balder also combines resurrection and immortality. All living things had promised not to harm him – except, that is, for mistletoe, which was considered too insignificant. The gods would amuse themselves by firing arrows at Balder, but, despite his apparent invulnerability, he was killed by a dart made of mistletoe. Hel promised that he could return to the land of the living if all things wept for him. All did, except one giantess, who responded: 'Let Hel keep her own!' The giantess was the trickster Loki in disguise, who was later punished. After the destruction of Ragnarok, it is expected that Balder will be reborn.

OPPOSITE *Anubis prepares the mummy of a dead worker for the next life.*
ABOVE *The Churning of the Ocean of Milk produced the nectar of eternal life.*

ABOVE *After Christ's resurrection, he ascended into heaven, witnessed by his disciples.* OPPOSITE *One of Christ's most spectacular miracles was raising Lazarus from the dead.*

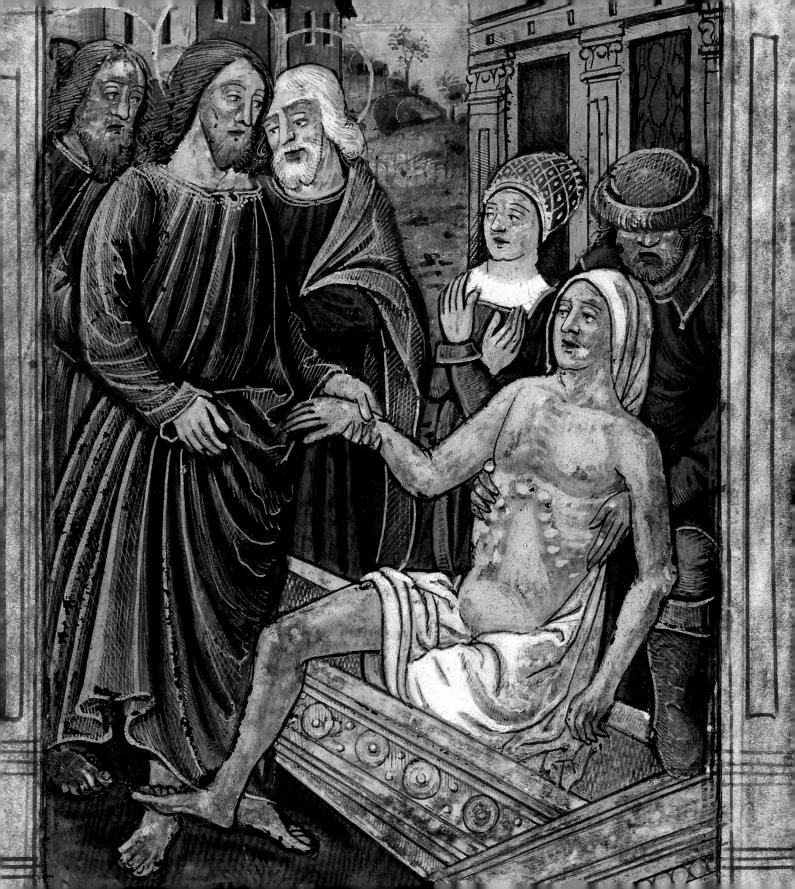

4

GIFTS FROM
||||||||||||||||||||||||||||||||||||||||
THE GODS
||||||||||||||||||||||||||||||||||||||||

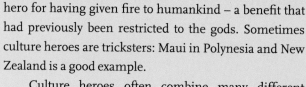

All mythology is concerned, directly or indirectly, with humans and with the roots that particular cultures share. Many myths attempt to explain not only who we are, but also the origins of society and civilization. This section considers how mythology has shaped humanity, society and religion.

One of the most common characters in world mythologies is the so-called 'culture hero': a person, god or creature who has given humanity gifts or taught us skills. The ancient Greek figure of Prometheus, for instance, is seen as a culture hero for having given fire to humankind – a benefit that had previously been restricted to the gods. Sometimes culture heroes are tricksters: Maui in Polynesia and New Zealand is a good example.

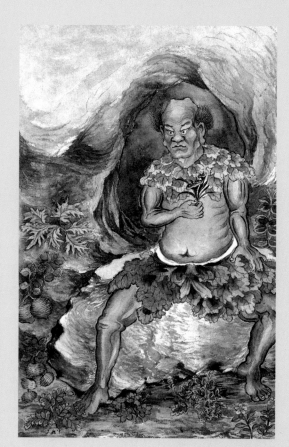

Culture heroes often combine many different roles. For example, the semi-mythical Chinese emperor Shennong was not only founder of an imperial dynasty, but also taught his people farming. In fact, Shennong – whose name means 'divine farmer' – was said to have tasted hundreds of different herbs in order to assess their medical value. A book attributed to him, *The Divine Farmer's Herb-Root Classic*, is generally considered to be the earliest work on Chinese medicine. He was also said to have discovered tea. As with many culture heroes, he straddles the line between reality and fantasy.

The Shennong legend reveals the fundamental importance of agriculture to civilization, as humankind began to take control of the land and settle into fixed communities. Many mythologies link cultivation to a particular god. In Greek mythology this was Demeter, who later became the Roman Ceres (from which we get the English word 'cereals'). There are also figures such as Triptolemus who are credited with bringing humans wheat. The Maya god Viracocha was another prolific culture hero. Walking among humans disguised as a beggar, he instructed on geometry, architecture, agriculture and astronomy. The Egyptian god Thoth, meanwhile, was credited with inventing writing, astronomy and astrology, and it was believed that Cadmus introduced writing to Greece.

The gods have also given us the arts. The Greeks and Romans attributed poetic skill to the Muses, who varied in number between three and nine, while in the *Prose Edda* poetry emerges from a war between the two godly tribes of the Aesir and the

PRECEDING PAGES *The shepherd–prince Paris had to choose the most beautiful goddess. Would it be Aphrodite, Athena or Hera?* LEFT *Shennong, the Chinese deity of medicine and agriculture. Dressed in leaves, he holds a plant with medicinal properties.* OPPOSITE *Cain and Abel: a classic story of sibling rivalry, ending in the latter's death.*

Vanir. To sign the truce, both spat into a cauldron; from this liquid a man called Kvasir emerged, and from his blood came the mead of poetry.

The role of alcohol in human society has special significance across various mythologies. Dionysus, the Greek god of the grape harvest, celebrated the consumption of wine, and his elderly companion Silenus was permanently drunk. In medieval Europe, Cain, the son of Adam, was believed to have invented alcohol.

Cain is perhaps best known for having committed the ultimate sin of murdering his brother. One important function of mythology (and religion) is to explain and support the laws of a society, especially if they can be shown to have divine origins. God gave the Ten Commandments directly to Moses, just as the laws of ancient Mesopotamia were supposedly passed from the gods directly to its rulers. The contravention of laws results in punishment (both on earth and in the afterlife), of which mythology offers many salutary examples.

Aside from strong leadership and clear systems of justice, complex societies rely on skilled craftsmen – and once more mythology offers prototyes. Hephaestus, one of the Olympian gods, was a blacksmith, and manufactured Hermes' winged sandals, Achilles' armour, Eros' bow and arrows, all of the gods' thrones, and even moulded Pandora out of earth. Curiously, he suffered the same lameness that afflicted earthly blacksmiths (caused by working with arsenic).

OPPOSITE *Tantalus, up to his neck in water he cannot drink, reaches in vain for the apples above him. He was punished for murdering his son and serving him up to the gods.* ABOVE *Sekhmet, the Egyptian goddess of divine retribution. The other lion-headed goddess, Bastet, was a goddess of fertility.* ABOVE RIGHT *Thoth and Horus pouring the water of life over Ptolemy XII.*

This chapter also looks at how myths have depicted certain abstract qualities – love and beauty, for instance, but also the sin of hubris, or excessive pride, in the eyes of the gods. The archangel Satan was punished for his presumption by being cast into hell; God destroyed mankind's ambitions embodied by the Tower of Babel; and when the Greek princess Niobe claimed that she was superior to Leto because she had more children, Apollo and Artemis – Leto's divine offspring – murdered her sons and daughters.

In return for the blessings from above, the gods have always expected something in return. Here we also look at the ways in which humanity has attempted to interact with the gods, most commonly in the form of worship and sacrifice. The Old Testament God was prepared to make Abraham sacrifice his son, Isaac, while the Aztecs would go to war in order to maintain the necessary stream of human sacrifices for their gods.

Agriculture

The Greek goddess Demeter is believed to have given Triptolemus wheat seeds and a chariot of dragons so that he might spread the benefits of agriculture around the world. In the Dogon tradition of Africa, the twins known as *Nummo* taught farming to humankind.

Elsewhere, agricultural gods reflect the type of crops grown locally. In the Americas we find a large range of maize gods. The Maya maize god often appears with the Hero Twins and is sometimes identified with their father, Hun Hunahpu. The story telling how the Twins retrieved their father's remains from the underworld suggests a link to the acquisition of agriculture; some also see him as a god of death and resurrection, reflecting the annual crop cycle. Maize was later used as an offering to Quetzalcoatl. In Shinto tradition, the rice god was Inari, who was always accompanied by messenger foxes. In the Philippines, the Ifugao people leave statues of the rice god Bulul to protect the crop.

One story relates that, as he watched a ploughing ceremony, the Buddha was struck by how hard the bull and farmer worked. Saddened, he entered his First Meditation on Life's Sorrows.

LEFT *Triptolemus sits in the winged chariot that he used to spread grain around the world.* BELOW *The Philippine figure of Bulul protects seeds and the harvest.* OPPOSITE *Two Navajo 'holy people' offer the sacred maize plant to humankind.*

Kingship

Many earthly kings themselves have claimed divine origins. Chinese mythology in particular blurs the line between history and legend, tracing kingship back to the Three Sovereigns: the semi-divine Fuxi, Shennong and Huang Di, who allegedly ruled in the 3rd millennium BC. Huang Di (the 'Yellow Emperor'), supposedly taught the Chinese farming, the taming of animals and how to build shelters.

In Korean tradition, Dangun – son of the ruler of heaven, Hwanung – descended to earth to bring culture to mankind. Tradition states that the first Japanese emperor was Jimmu, who traced his ancestry back to Izanagi (see p. 129) and Amaterasu (see p. 42).

In Egypt, Osiris was both a god and the first pharaoh, while in Mesopotamia each city had its own foundation myth and its own first ruler; the mythical hero Gilgamesh appears on the Sumerian King List, which dates to about 2100 BC. The first Inca king, Manco Capac, was believed to be descended from the creator god Viracocha through his son, the sun god Inti.

LEFT *The hero Gilgamesh was almost certainly modelled on a real-life king.* ABOVE *Fuxi was acknowledged as the first emperor of China, as well as the inventor of writing, marriage, fishing and animal husbandry.* OPPOSITE *Dangun was the legendary first king of Korea, said to be descended from the gods.*

Laws and Justice

All mythologies have something to say about the origins of law and codes for living. For example, several books of the Old Testament – in particular Deuteronomy and Exodus – incorporate extensive lists of rules. The Bible describes how Moses received the Ten Commandments – for Jews and Christians, the most fundamental principles outlining moral and religious behaviour – directly from God, on the summit of Mount Sinai. Returning to the Israelites, he discovered them worshipping a golden calf (see p. 254), and in his rage smashed the tablets on which the laws were inscribed – before returning to the mountain top to get another set.

In Hinduism the *Manusmriti*, or 'Laws of Manu', is a discourse supposedly delivered by Manu, the first human. It explains the concept of *dharma*: the eternal law of the cosmos, and each individual's religious and social obligations. In Mesopotamian mythology the cosmic laws were supposedly guarded by Ishtar. After raping Ninlil, the god Enlil was judged by a court made up of fifty great gods and seven decision-makers; he was punished by being sent to the underworld.

OPPOSITE *The Buddhist figure of Ksitigarbha, who dispenses justice to souls in the underworld.* BELOW *Moses shows the divine tablets inscribed with the Ten Commandments to the Israelites.*

ABOVE LEFT *Hammurabi, the king of Babylon, is given law tablets by the sun god Shamash.* LEFT *A cylinder-seal impression showing a bound bird-man, Zu, judged by the seated Enki (also known as Ea). He was accused of attempting to steal the 'tablet of destiny'.*

Only through divine law – symbolized by the two central tablets – can Christians hope to break death's iron grip.

War

For ancient civilizations such as Greece, Egypt and Mesopotamia, war was a part of everyday life. Wars also feature heavily in mythological epics. The drawn-out Trojan War eventually launched the adventures of Aeneas and Odysseus, while the *Mahabharata* ends with the almighty Kurukshetra War, between two dynastic groups.

Victory depended on winning the support of the gods of war. The armour-clad Mesopotamian goddess of war, Ishtar, was said to see it as a game. The Greeks had two main gods of war, Ares (ruthless and brutal) and Athena (strategic and tactical). Other deities were more specialized: Hachiman was the Shinto–Buddhist god of instruction in warfare, and the Norse god Tyr was the patron of single combat. Others offered inspiration to warriors: the Hindu goddess Durga – an avatar of Devi – for instance, who maintained patience and courage on the battlefield. The Irish Morrígan was a goddess of the battlefield, taking the form of a crow.

The most fearsome war deity was perhaps the lion-headed Sekhmet (see p. 171). She was bloodthirsty and savage, and the Egyptians held an annual festival in her honour, to pacify her.

In Aztec mythology war was practically a religious obligation. Tezcatlipoca, the warrior god, saw it as his job to provoke wars, thus ensuring a steady flow of captives – who might later be sacrificed to the gods.

ABOVE *Durga being armed by other Hindu gods.* OPPOSITE *A Persian depiction of Mars, who holds a two-bladed sword, a trident, a dagger and a club.*

بیوروز که روز سنت ازاین است
در اول روز زیت که بحمل می آید
صورت بیج حمل است

حمل وعقرب بتعلق بمرخ دارد

وخاکی وتخ وکل ش کرست وکال حندر بر جست که هفتم او وقت

OPPOSITE *Love (Venus) here overcomes War (Mars). Cupid unties Mars' sandals.* RIGHT *Durga slays the Buffalo Demon.*

Fire

The discovery and control of fire was a great breakthrough for humanity, distinguishing us from the animals, and providing warmth and the means to cook. Inevitably, there are many stories on how humans acquired this advantage.

In Greek mythology the Titan Prometheus stole fire from the gods by hiding it in a reed (provoking the wrath of Zeus in the process). His story finds parallels elsewhere in the world. In Polynesia, for example, fire was stolen for humanity by the culture hero Maui (see p. 70), while in Brazil it was the young hero Botoque who took fire from the jaguars.

There are many gods of fire. Xiuhtecuhtli is the Aztec 'lord of fire' (and god of turquoise). In Japan, the Shinto fire god is Kagutsuchi, the son of the first couple, Izanagi and Izanami. Sadly, his birth resulted in his mother's fiery death. His father, furious, cut off his son's head, and a new generation of gods sprang out.

The Hindu god of fire, Agni, is often depicted with two or three heads, suggesting that his gift is something of a mixed blessing. Some legends say that he was the first son of the great creator god Brahma.

Fire is also associated with mythological creatures, from the dragon to the salamander (which appeared to be born from the flames) and the phoenix (which would spontaneously combust, only to rise once again from the ashes).

OPPOSITE LEFT
*Xiuhtecuhtli, the
Aztec 'lord of fire'.*
OPPOSITE RIGHT *A
statue of the Hindu
fire god, Agni.* RIGHT
*Flame-headed Agni
astride his goat.*

Bardel

Lith. de C Motte.

ABOVE *The Aztec fire ceremony, in which four priests are burning 'year bundles'.*
OPPOSITE *Without fire there is no life: Prometheus descends to man with his precious gift.*

Love and Beauty

The Greek god of love, Eros, was one of the earliest to have been born, allowing all the other gods to procreate. The most beautiful Greek goddess, however, was Aphrodite (Venus to the Romans) – a reputation confirmed by the so-called Judgment of Paris. According to myth, a wedding was held to which Eris – the goddess of discord – was not invited. Angered, she threw into the wedding party a golden apple with the inscription: 'To the fairest'. Three goddesses – Athena, Hera and Aphrodite – argued as to who should receive it, until Zeus called the Trojan mortal Paris to judge. Paris chose Aphrodite, angering the other two. As a bribe, Aphrodite had promised Paris the love of the world's most beautiful woman. She was already married, however – her name was Helen (of Troy) – and the outcome of Paris's decision was the Trojan War (see p. 320).

The perils of beauty are underlined in the Classical tale of Narcissus. This handsome youth was extremely proud of his looks and disdained all romantic interest, so the gods made him fall in love with his own image, reflected in a pond. Unable to leave the spot, he wasted away.

The Aztec Xochipilli was the god of both love and beauty, while his sister, Xochiquetzal, stood for female beauty in particular. They were the patrons of male and female prostitutes.

LEFT *Xochipilli, the Aztec god of flowers, was also considered to be the god of love.* RIGHT *The Japanese Buddhist god Aizen Myo-o represents passion. His flaming hair stands for uncontrolled lust.* OPPOSITE *Eros pursues the huntress Atalanta. He holds a whip, perhaps symbolizing the hardships of love.*

A tale of unrequited
love. The wood nymph
Echo is doomed to
love the self-absorbed
Narcissus.

The One Thousand and One Nights contains a number of stories about love. Here, Sayf Ul-Maluk and Badi'a al-Jamal, the first a prince, the latter a jinn or demon, have overcome their different backgrounds to be together. They are carried aloft by more jinn.

Fate and Fortune

The concepts of fate and fortune are attempts to explain the sometimes random events that befall us. In myths they play an important role, and sometimes a hero finds himself fighting against a curse or prediction. The story of Oedipus is a good example: in spite of the extraordinary care he took, he ended up killing his father and marrying his mother, as had been predicted.

The ancient Greeks believed that each individual's destiny was determined at birth by three spinning women known as the Fates (Moirai), called Clotho, Lachesis and Atropos. Their Norse equivalents were the Norns – three women who visited each newborn child to decide what sort of life it would have.

The story of Meleager proves that nobody could escape the Fates. It was prophesied that his life would end when a particular piece of wood was burned. Meleager's mother decided to cheat fate by hiding the wood in a chest, but in later life used it to make a fire; her son died instantly.

For the Romans, luck was personified by the goddess Fortuna. Gods of luck are also found in Japan and China. The Andean cultures were keen on divination: just as the Greeks visited the oracle at Delphi, the Inca had a soothsayer at Pachacamac, who was a mouthpiece perhaps for their principal god, Viracocha.

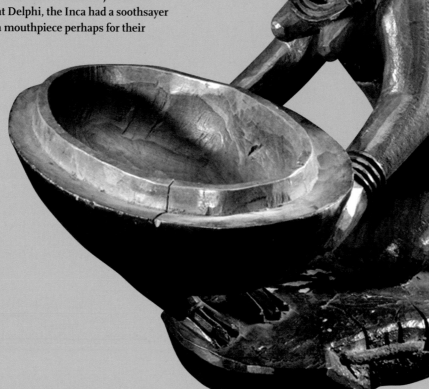

RIGHT *A Yoruba bowl used for divination.* OPPOSITE *Japanese folklore recognizes seven gods of good fortune.*

Music

Music's calming properties are well recognized in mythology (Hermes uses it to put the ferocious Cerberus to sleep, for instance), but it can also lead to conflict. The satyr Marsyas challenged the god Apollo to a musical competition – and was flayed alive for his presumption. King Midas was witness to another musical contest – between Apollo and Pan, who had fashioned the first pan pipes out of reeds – but unwisely favoured the latter's performance. His reward was a pair of ass's ears.

The Chinese immortal Fuxi, who travelled between heaven and earth, taught men to play a simple stringed instrument. According to Chinese myth, the lute was invented by the legendary emperor Di Ku; when played, it made even pheasants and phoenixes dance.

In Greek myth, the inventor of the lyre was the infant Hermes, though its greatest player was Apollo. The Old Testament King David was also an accomplished harpist, as well as the composer of the Psalms. Harps appear frequently in Norse and Celtic mythology, and the German epic *Nibelungenlied* tells of how King Gunther, when thrown into a snake pit with his hands bound, continued to play the instrument with his feet.

A rattle called a *sistrum* was used in the worship of the Egyptian goddess Hathor, who is often depicted holding one. In Aztec mythology the god of music was Xochipilli.

ABOVE *Krishna and Radha dancing in the rain with three musicians.* OPPOSITE *The legendary Irish poet Ossian evokes the spirits of Celtic mythology through his playing.*

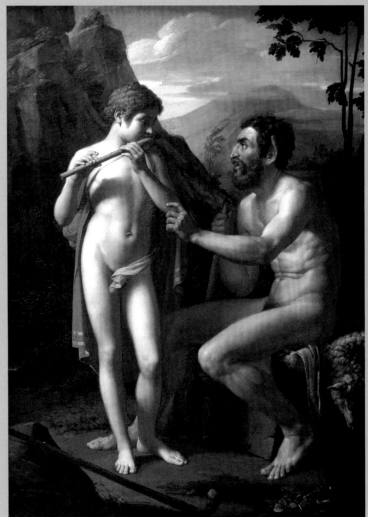

ABOVE LEFT *King David was a gifted harpist, and is traditionally credited with the composition of the Psalms.* ABOVE *The satyr Marsyas teaches the young musician Olympus to play the flute.* OPPOSITE *Orpheus charms the animals with his music.*

Sacrifice

Sacrifice involves offering plants, animals or even humans to gods, spirits or ancestors (the last is a common tradition in China and Japan).

For the Aztecs, human sacrifice was necessary to sustain the sun. The Germanic peoples also practised human sacrifice, by hanging (in imitation of Odin: see p. 152) and drowning (see p. 112). The feud between Cain and Abel began when Cain's offering of grain was rejected by God, while Abel's animal sacrifice was accepted.

It was said that Prometheus tricked Zeus by offering him two types of sacrifice – one consisting of meat inside a stomach, and the other an animal's bone wrapped in skin and fat. Zeus chose the bones and skin, thus establishing the rule for future sacrifices: humans ate the meat and burned the bones. In Hinduism, Agni, the fire god, carries sacrifices to the gods.

There were limits to the gods' demands. The Old Testament God tested Abraham by demanding that he sacrifice his son, Isaac, but just before the deed sent Abraham a ram instead. And when Lycaon sacrificed a human child, Zeus turned him into a wolf.

BELOW *Abraham is about to sacrifice his son, Isaac, but an angel stops him.* OPPOSITE *A romanticized recreation of the rites involved in the Roman worship of Isis.*

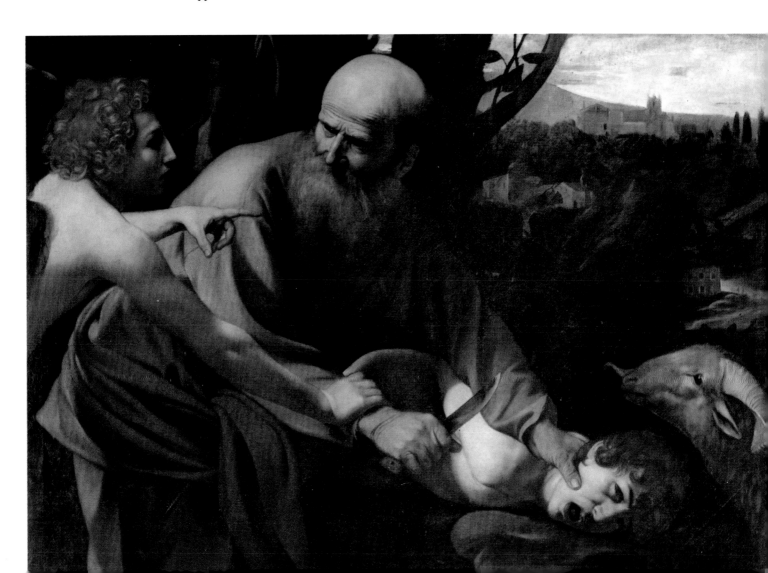

Folly

|||||||||||||||||||||||||||||

Humanity's attempts to outdo the gods have always ended in disaster. A good example is the biblical story of the Tower of Babel, which the Book of Genesis describes as a tower reaching to heaven. God, furious with its builders for their hubris, confused their language; the workers were no longer unable to communicate with each other, and the project was abandoned.

Another example is the story of Daedalus, designer of the Minotaur's labyrinth. King Minos would not let him leave Crete, so Daedalus fashioned wings for him and his son, Icarus, out of wax and feathers. Icarus ignored his father's warnings not to get too close to the sun, his wings melted, and he fell to his death.

ABOVE *Lycaon offered Zeus a child as a sacrifce and was turned into a wolf for his hubris.* OPPOSITE *Escaping from Crete with his father, Icarus flew too close to the sun and fell into the sea.*

LEFT *Three characters from Greek mythology and their punishments: Sisyphus carrying a boulder, Ixion tied to a wheel and Tantalus attempting to drink water.* BELOW *Loki had his lips sewn shut as a punishment.* OPPOSITE *An angel leads a new soul into hell.*

Punishment

For the Greeks, Tartarus was a section of the underworld reserved for punishment. There, Sisyphus was forced to push a boulder up a hill for ever, while Tantalus was kept in state of permanent hunger and thirst. The Christian vision of hell shares many characteristics with Tartarus.

The Norse prankster-god Loki was frequently in trouble. On one occasion, Loki had commissioned some magical objects (including Odin's spear) from a group of dwarfs, the Sons of Ivaldi. Loki declared these smiths to be without equal, but the dwarf Brokk wagered that he could produce even more impressive objects, and so fashioned Thor's hammer, Mjölnir. When Brokk went to claim his prize – Loki's head – Loki said that he could have his head, but had no claim on his neck. Brokk instead sewed up the wily god's lips with a leather cord.

5

THE ANIMAL
||||||||||||||||||||||||||||||||||||||||||||
KINGDOM
||||||||||||||||||||||||||||||||||||||||

Humans are central to the mythologies they have created, but they are not the only creatures on earth. Indeed, many myths are at pains to distinguish humanity from the animal kingdom. Although, according to the Bible, God created the animals before humans, he decided that a higher being was required to keep order over everything.

Not all traditions subscribed to that view. Native Americans did and do believe that all of us originated from animals, and that an animal's spirit is in every way comparable to our own. Cheyenne mythology tells of a time when animals could talk to humans. The buffalo insisted that they were the equals of humans, so a race was organized. Two teams were formed: one of a buffalo, a deer and an antelope, the other of a human, a dog, a hawk and an eagle. The latter group won, whereafter dogs became man's best friend, and eagles and hawks gained our respect. The other animals were now to be hunted.

Animal worship began early in human history: certainly people were recognizing animal and anthropomorphic gods by around 30,000 BC, as suggested by the small statue of a lion-man found in the cave of Hohlenstein-Stadel, Germany, and dating from that period. The most powerful predators in any particular area were usually venerated: there was jaguar worship in Mesoamerica, lion worship in Egypt, and bear worship among the Sami in Finland and Native North Americans. The Ainu of Japan would sacrifice bears, sometimes raising them from young cubs. Snakes, universally feared, are perhaps the most commonly occurring animals in myth; scorpions, too, appear repeatedly in West Asian and Egyptian mythology. With time, animal gods gradually gave way to animal–human deities, such as those found in ancient Egypt and Mesopotamia.

Animal–human hybrids are staples of Greek and Roman legend – well-known creatures including the Minotaur, centaurs, harpies, sphinxes, chimeras and sirens. In Hinduism, the best-known animal–human deity is perhaps the elephant-headed god Ganesha. Various tales are told of how he acquired this form, but one describes how his father, Shiva, cut off his original head in anger, and then

replaced it with that of the first animal he saw. The gods of Mexico and South America often have fluid animal forms: Quetzalcoatl, for example, literally means 'plumed serpent'. Sometimes the creatures chosen for veneration were surprising. For instance, one of the most ubiquitous symbols in ancient Egypt was the scarab dung beetle: the insect rolling its ball of dung was compared to the sun god Khepri guiding the celestial sphere across the sky.

Domestication and animal husbandry were closely linked to human society. The first species to be domesticated was probably the dog, some 15,000 years ago, followed soon after by sheep. Meat, wool and leather all come from animals and were viewed as gifts from the gods. One Native American myth maintains that all game animals were originally trapped in a cave; humans had only to open the door and shoot what they needed. One day, however, the animals escaped, and now humans must go hunting for their prey.

Sometimes animals were instrumental in creating and nurturing humankind. In Norse mythology the cow Audumla licked the first humans into shape from a block of salt. According to Greek legend, Zeus, hidden as an infant in a cave, was raised by the goat Amalthea. The Phrygian Mother goddess Cybele was brought up by wild animals, while Romulus and Remus were suckled by a she-wolf, and the infant Atalanta by a bear. In such cases their rough upbringing gave the deity or hero an immediate connection to nature.

Animals are often associated with particular gods. Zeus is linked with eagles, and Odin, his Norse counterpart, with wolves and ravens. The Hindu gods have a range of sentient animal mounts: Ganesha is depicted on the back of a mouse, while others ride peacocks, bulls and tigers. Aphrodite is sometimes depicted riding a goose or swan, while Dionysus' chariot is pulled by tigers.

Occasionally animals can prove wily and deceitful. In Native North American tradition, Coyote and Raven are both tricksters. In Japan no one trusts foxes (least of all the old ones with several tails, since they are shape-shifters). Animals could, in fact, lead to downfall: a snake in the Garden of Eden tempted the first humans into sin, and a giant wooden horse fooled the Trojans into welcoming hidden Greek troops into their city, leading to its destruction at the end of a ten-year siege.

OPPOSITE Animals have particular significance in Aboriginal mythology, particularly in the Dreamtime. RIGHT *The Persian simurgh – a beast related to the equally mythical roc – leads an army of birds.*

Cows and Bulls

The bull cult is one of the oldest in Indo-European culture. It stretches back as far as Mesopotamia: the *Epic of Gilgamesh* tells how the sky god Anu controlled a creature known as the Bull of Heaven, which was sent to kill Gilgamesh. Bulls' crescent-shaped horns led them to be associated with the moon.

In ancient Egypt, the bull god Apis was important initially as a fertility god, and later as a protector of the dead. It is thought that the biblical golden calf worshipped by the Israelites in the wilderness was an extension of the Apis cult. Apis's female counterpart was the cow Hathor, who suckled the infant Horus.

Archaeological evidence shows that another early bull cult was located on Crete, though little is known about its exact nature. Legend states that the Minotaur was the product of a match between Pasiphaë, the wife of the Cretan King Minos, and a white bull that emerged from the sea. Aphrodite caused Pasiphaë to fall in love with the bull, and Daedalus (see p. 200) built a device to allow the queen to mate with it.

This was not the only bovine-related romance in Greek myth. There is another legend that Zeus turned himself into a beautiful white bull in order to seduce Europa. Another story tells how Zeus, to avoid Hera discovering his liaison, turned the nypmh Io into a heifer. When his wife found out, she sent a gadfly to chase her to the ends of the earth. The modern-day Bosphorus in Turkey literally means 'cow crossing', since Io was believed to have crossed into Asia there.

Norse mythology maintained that humanity began with the cow Audumla, who licked the first humans out of salt. Four rivers of milk flowed from her udders, reminding us of the four rivers of Paradise.

Cows remain sacred to Hindus today. The bull Nandi is ridden by Shiva and is the gatekeeper of the god's residence, as well as being his first supporter.

RIGHT *A curious double-headed Egyptian bust merging the Roman god Antinous with the bull god Apis.* OPPOSITE *Shiva and Parvati ride the bull mount Nandi.*

OPPOSITE *A scene from an Egyptian painted coffin shows the bull as a god of creation and rebirth.* ABOVE RIGHT *An unusual depiction of the Minotaur, in which just its torso is human.* RIGHT *A bull on the Ishtar Gate, from ancient Babylon.*

LEFT *The Hindu concept of the Sacred Cow, source of all prosperity and in which all the gods are said to reside.* OPPOSITE *Daedalus produces a wooden cow that will allow Pasiphaë to copulate with her favourite bull.*

Tigers, Lions and Jaguars

As dominant predators, big cats feature prominently in mythology. Lions in particular are associated with deities. The Babylonian deity Nergal is often portrayed as a lion, while the Egyptian goddesses Sekhmet and Bastet each have a lion's head, as does the god of war, Maahes. The goddesses Hera and Cybele had chariots drawn by lions, and Hindu temples contain images of a powerful, magical lion called a *yali*, which is sometimes depicted with elephant tusks.

Lions make fearsome adversaries. Heracles' first task was to defeat the Nemean Lion, which was famous for having an invincible skin, so he strangled the animal instead. He then cut off the lion's skin using the creature's own claws and wore it. In the Old Testament, Daniel is saved by God from death in the lions' den.

The jaguar is central to Aztec and Maya mythology, being associated with the god Tezcatlipoca and his Maya counterpart, Ahau Kin. For the Maya, jaguars could travel between the living and the dead, and protected the royal family. The early Olmec civilization also depicted a type of were-jaguar in its art, similar to the European werewolf. The Aztecs had jaguar-warriors, who dressed in imitation of the animals.

In Hinduism a tiger called Dawon was the occasional mount of Durga; in Chinese mythology too the tiger is sometimes a mount for gods, and also the dragon's rival.

OPPOSITE *Korean mountain spirits are often accompanied by tigers.*
ABOVE *This plate from Afghanistan shows Cybele in her lion-drawn chariot.*

ਹਰਬੜਿਨਾਜਤ · ਝਾਇਰਿਰਤਸਿਪੁਰਕਟਝ ਫਰੇਸਾਐ ਪ੍ਰੇਸਰ—   ਵਜਮੈ ਤੁਰਪ੍ਰੈਸਅਪਿ ਹ ਤਝਸਰ

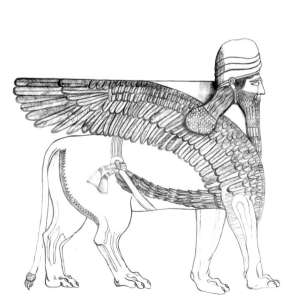

ABOVE *Durga rides on the back of a tiger.* LEFT *A strange lion–human hybrid from the city of Nineveh.* RIGHT *The jaguar occupies an important position in Aztec mythology and inspired a band of warriors.*

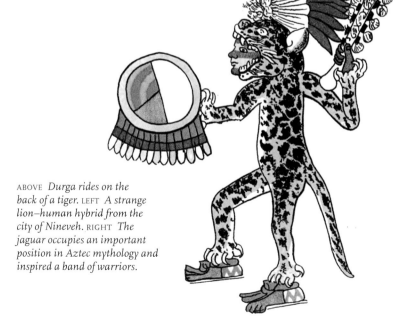

A Chinese
protector-deity,
accompanied
by a tiger.

趙公明紂之猛將能伏大虎

Eagles

Eagles are often associated with gods and royalty. The Sumerian king Etana, wanting a son, was sent an eagle by the sun god Shamash. The eagle carried Etana to heaven, where the goddess Ishtar accepted his petition, and thus the first Sumerian dynasty was founded. The Mesopotamian Anzu bird, a lion–eagle hybrid, caused storms with its wings.

Likewise, Native American mythology includes the Thunderbird, whose beating wings cause thunder and whose eyes flash lightning. Some myths describe Eagle as the Thunderbird's assistant. In Mexico, the Aztecs' elite troops were the eagle warriors, soldiers of the sun.

In Greek mythology the eagle was one of Zeus´ favourite guises – used, for instance, when he abducted Ganymede (see p. 140). In Hindu mythology Garuda, the king of the birds and often Vishnu's mount, was part eagle.

The top of the Norse World Tree, Yggdrasil, was home to an eagle who understood the workings of the universe. In Celtic mythology eagles are the second oldest animal (after the salmon), and in the Welsh *Mabinogion* the wise eagle helps the hero find the magical child Mabon.

OPPOSITE ABOVE *This Native American headdress depicts the Thunderbird.* OPPOSITE BELOW *Vishnu astride the mythical Garuda.* ABOVE *An elite Aztec eagle warrior. The eagle was a symbol of the sun.*

An ancient Greek cup showing Zeus with his emblem, an eagle.

The Thunderbird, creator of storms, hurls lightning bolts on this Pawnee ceremonial drum.

Ravens

The most famous ravens in mythology are probably Huginn and Muninn, which sat on Odin's shoulders. These two birds acted as his messengers, bringing him information about the entire world. In Celtic mythology they were associated with war.

Ravens also play the role of heavenly messengers in the Bible. In the Old Testament, God sent a raven to feed the prophet Elijah, and according to the Koran God sent a raven to dig Abel's grave after he had been killed by his brother, Cain. The Talmud describes the raven as one of three species that copulated while on Noah's Ark. Once the flood was over, Noah sent out a raven

and a dove. The raven got lost, while the dove returned with an olive twig in its beak.

In Native American mythology Raven is a trickster figure, a little like Coyote (see p. 70). According to some legends he created the world, his droppings becoming the mountains. He also took salacious delight in teaching humanity how to reproduce.

ABOVE *The Old Testament prophet Elijah being fed by a raven while hiding in the wilderness.* OPPOSITE *Odin's two ravens – Huginn and Muninn – perch on his shoulders and give him counsel. Note the god's missing eye.*

UPTRAETQVINDECICVBITISALCIORI
SVPTRECTOISCROSVPTRAEMISNOECO
BT

TELLEXNOEXCESSASETQDILVVII:
VINNVBIB: ETERITSIGNVFEOD

OPPOSITE *Noah released two birds after the Flood. The first, a raven, went to feast on carrion, whereas the dove returned with an olive branch.*
TOP *This Native American shaman's rattle shows a raven carrying the moon in its beak.*
ABOVE *This curious shamanic carving from Greenland is part raven, part dead child.*

Peacocks

The peacock is associated with Zeus' wife, Hera, and is often shown drawing her chariot (a popular motif in the Renaissance). The bird got its distinctive tail from Hera, too: her son, the hundred-eyed giant Argus, was beheaded by Apollo, but Hera placed his eyes in the peacock's tail.

In Christian tradition the peacock became associated with the Virgin Mary, as a symbol of purity. Peacocks are also used as mounts by various Hindu deities, including the goddess Saraswati. They are said to represent pride, though in other contexts they can stand for immortality.

ABOVE *The hundred-eyed Argus was entrusted with guarding Io. After he had been slain by Hermes, Hera put his eyes in the peacock's tail.* OPPOSITE *A Mozarabic illustration of a peacock, from a 10th-century Bible.*

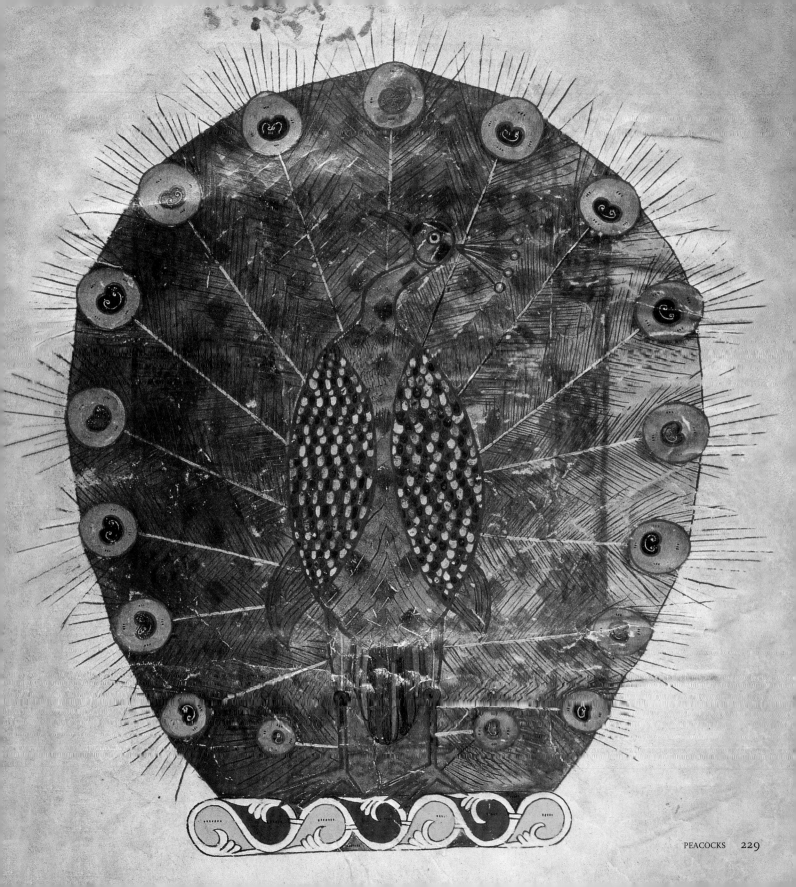

ABOVE *A scene from a fable by Jean de La Fontaine, in which the peacock complains about its grating voice to a statue of the goddess Hera – with whom the bird was closely associated.* OPPOSITE *The Hindu river goddess Saraswati is normally depicted with her peacock.*

Snakes

Snakes are one of humankind's oldest adversaries. Some scholars have suggested that, in myth, they stand as phallic symbols, while others have associated them with earth mothers (since they live in the ground).

The most infamous serpent in the Judaeo-Christian tradition is that which appears in the Garden of Eden. God punishes it by forcing it to crawl upon its belly – which would suggest that it originally had legs. Later, Moses created a brazen snake that miraculously cured snakebites.

In other mythologies snakes can take on gigantic proportions: Apollo battled against the mighty Python (a sort of dragon, though usually depicted as a snake), while the Norse god Thor fought against the greatest of all snakes, the Midgard Serpent. This creature, also known as the World Snake, coiled itself around the entire globe.

Not all snakes are bad, however. Quetzalcoatl, one of the most important Mesoamerican culture heroes, is frequently depicted as a 'feathered serpent'; and in Hindu mythology the giant, multiheaded snake Shesha (also called Ananta, 'without end') subserviently supports Vishnu as he sleeps between bouts of creation. The Naga snakes are the sworn enemies of Garuda, the mount of Vishnu.

ABOVE *An image of the Egyptian Sata snake from a Book of the Dead.* RIGHT *Garuda, the eagle of wisdom and enemy of the Naga (serpents).* OPPOSITE *The legendary king Gunnar (Gunther) was thrown into a snake pit – as in this 9th-century Scandinavian carving.*

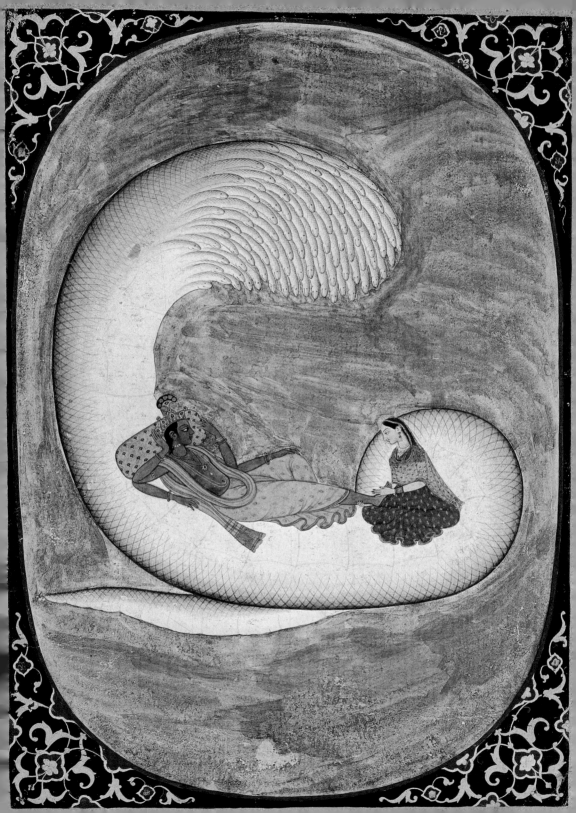

OPPOSITE *The many-headed serpent Shesha was said to be Vishnu's most devoted follower.* RIGHT *God's punishment for the serpent who tempted Eve was that it should crawl on its belly and eat dust.*

Goats

Goats are one of our oldest domesticated species, a fact that might account for their prominence in European myth. The infant Zeus, for instance – hiding from his father in a cave on Mount Ida, Crete – was raised by the goat Amalthea. Amalthea later presented him with one of her horns, filled with flowers and fruits (a cornucopia, or 'horn of plenty'). The Greek god Pan had the legs of a goat, and the ferocious mythical Chimera was said to have a goat's mid-section – along with parts of a lion and a dragon.

The chariot of the Norse god Thor was pulled by the goats Tanngrisnir and Tanngnjóstr, which he killed and cooked every night, but the following morning they were miraculously revived. Once Thor shared his meal with some peasants, one of whom broke a bone to eat the marrow – and the following day the goat was lame.

BELOW *Thor discovers that one of his goats is lame.* OPPOSITE *In this rowdy bacchanal, Pan's emblem, the goat, makes an appearance.*

Horses

From around 4000 BC, when horses were first domesticated, they have been an invaluable form of transport. Odin's horse, Sleipnir, had eight legs, making him fast and sure-footed (on occasion he even rode to the underworld). The offspring of Loki, he was sired when that trouble-making god was disguised as a mare.

The Greek centaurs were half-human, half-horse, whereas the winged horse Pegasus sprang from the monstrous Medusa's neck after Perseus had beheaded her. The hero Bellerophon later rode Pegasus to kill the Chimera.

Perhaps the most famous mythological horse was not a real horse at all. After years of laying siege to Troy, the Greeks pretended to go home, leaving an enormous offering in the form of a wooden horse. The Trojans accepted the gift, but were surprised to find it full of Greek soldiers.

ABOVE *The hero Bellerophon, mounted on the winged horse Pegasus, fights the Chimera.* OPPOSITE *In the course of his eighth labour, Heracles fed Diomedes of Thrace to his own carnivorous horses.*

Wolves

||||||||||||||||||||||||||||||||||||||||||

The giant wolf Fenrir, son of Loki, was the enemy of the Norse god Odin. He was captured by the gods, but they were unable to kill him, so they chained him up. Fenrir continues to grow, however, and by the time of Ragnarok will fill the space between earth and heaven. During the final battle he will devour Odin. Norse myth also includes tales of the giantess Hyrrokkin, who rode on a giant wolf, using reins made of vipers.

According to Native American mythology, an argument between Wolf and Coyote led to Wolf killing Coyote's son, thus introducing death into the world.

OPPOSITE *The hero Faramarz kills a witch-wolf – an animal from hell. An illustration, the Persian 'book of kings'.* ABOVE *A Native American ritual headdress in the form of a wolf.* RIGHT *The giant wolf Fenrir bites off the hand of the god Tyr.*

ABOVE *The Aztec god Macuilzochitl, in the form of a tortoise.* OPPOSITE TOP *Vishnu appears as his avatar Kurma, the tortoise.* OPPOSITE CENTRE *This Maya ceramic shows the creator of the world standing on a turtle, which represented the earth.* OPPOSITE BELOW *A Sioux amulet in the form of a turtle, worn to ward off illness.*

Turtles

The important role played by turtles and tortoises in world mythology is largely on account of their longevity. In Hinduism the turtle Akupara carries the world on its back (in some accounts it supports an elephant that, in turn, supports the world), whereas the giant turtle Kurma is instrumental in the Churning of the Ocean of Milk (see p. 162). The concept of the World Turtle also appears in some Native American myths, which attribute earthquakes to its movements.

In China the tortoise was said to have helped Pan Gu create the world. Another legend claims that, after Gong Gong destroyed the mountain that supported the sky, the creator goddess Nuwa propped the heavens with the legs of a giant turtle, Ao. It was also said that Ao carried Mount Penglai on its back.

African myths often depict the tortoise as the cleverest animal (a conclusion also reflected in Aesop's fables). In Greek mythology the infant Hermes fashioned the first harp from a tortoise shell strung with cow gut. The Aztecs also used turtle shells for music-making, which is why the animal frequently appears alongside Macuilzochitl, an aspect of Xochipilli, a god of music. And in Maya mythology there are tales of the maize god being reborn from the carapace of a turtle.

Mythological Creatures

Fantastical creatures that defy normal categorization appear in all mythologies. Most are composites of other animals or human–animal hybrids. They are not necessarily ill-intentioned, but most do have magical powers.

Perhaps the best-known example is that of the dragon. Originating in Mesopotamia, stories of this mythical beast spread to ancient Greece and to China and Japan. In Asia the dragon became an auspicious creature, a bringer of good fortune and a royal symbol. In Greece, however, it became more monstrous, something that heroes had to overcome.

The griffin – a combination of lion and eagle – can be found in the ancient Near East, and later on Crete. In Christian tradition the unicorn could be tamed only by a maiden, and came to be associated with the Virgin Mary. While the majority of Egyptian gods were animal–human hybrids, there were some who were composed solely of different animal parts: the demon Ammit, for example, combined crocodile, hippo and lion.

The Greek Sphinx had the body and legs of a lion, the wings of an eagle, and the head and torso of a woman. Its ancient Egyptian equivalent tended to be male – and more benevolent.

BELOW *Tales of dragons appeared all over the world. This woodcut illustrates a dragon supposedly found near Kraków, Poland.*
OPPOSITE *The Sphinx was a combination of lion, eagle and human. Here it poses its riddle to Oedipus.*

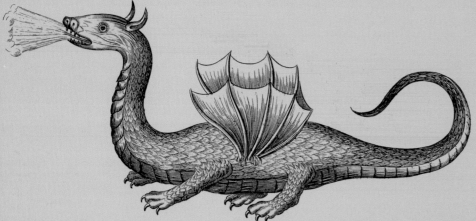

ABOVE LEFT *The centaur Chiron appears in the foreground of this fresco. In the centre is Mount Helicon, and the Hippocrene fountain created by Pegasus.* LEFT *A typical European fire-breathing dragon.* ABOVE *An early depiction of a Greek centaur, with prominent genitals and a threatening stance.* OPPOSITE *The hideous Egyptian demon Ammit, who combined hippo, lion and crocodile, and devoured the souls of the unworthy dead.*

Metamorphosis

In the 1st century AD the Roman poet Ovid gathered together a compendium of Classical stories involving shape-shifters. The universe he describes is fluid, and nothing is what it seems: the woman Arachne, who challenges Minerva to a weaving competition, is turned into a spider; Alcyone and her husband are turned into kingfishers; and Atalanta is turned into a lion.

Metamorphosis also crops up in Hindu tradition. One story tells of a demon king, Hiranyakashipu, who as a result of his devotion had obtained immortality: he could be killed by neither man nor beast. Vishnu's solution to this problem was simple: he transformed himself into the avatar Narasimha – half-man, half-lion – and in this form destroyed him.

ABOVE *As Minerva looks on, Arachne works at her loom, unaware of her forthcoming metamorphosis.* RIGHT *Shiva replaced the head of his child Ganesha with that of an elephant.* OPPOSITE *Hiranyakashipu, invincible by either man or beast, is devoured by the hybrid Narasimha.*

Actaeon's punishment for seeing Artemis bathing was to be turned into a stag – and killed by his own dogs. LEFT *Odysseus' companions were turned into various animals by the witch Circe.*

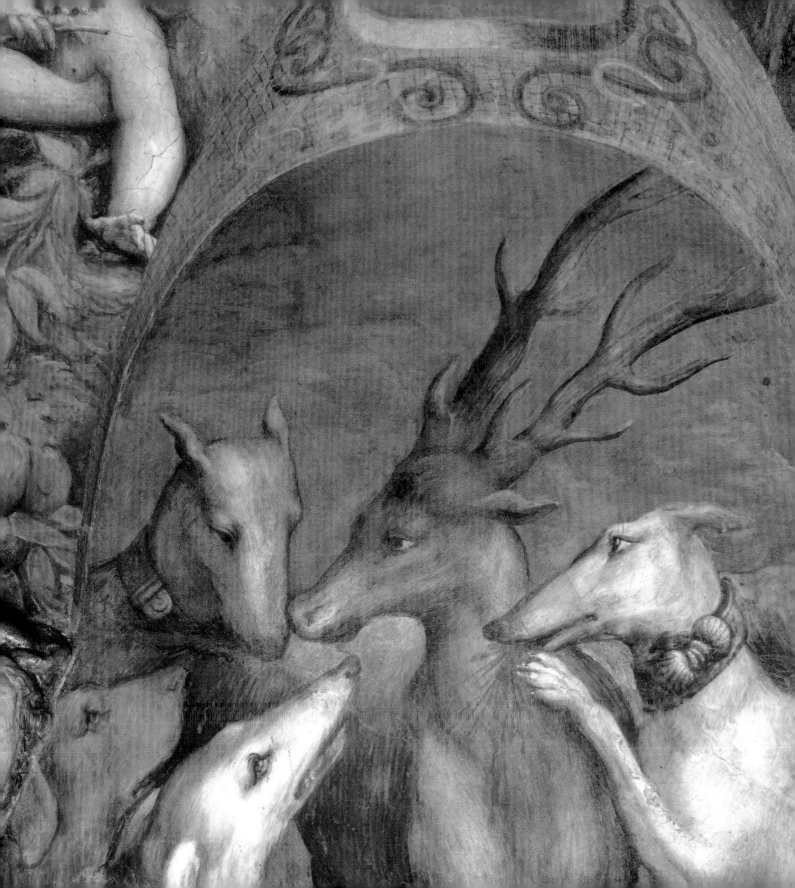

6

SYMBOLIC
IIIIIIIIIIIIIIIIIIIIIIIIIIIIIIIIIIIIIII
SUBSTANCES
IIIIIIIIIIIIIIIIIIIIIIIIIIIIIIIIIIIIIIIIII

Certain substances are charged with meaning in mythology: the materials of everyday existence, for instance, such as clay, blood, milk and fire. Others are less common, but universal and highly prized: a good example would be gold, which most cultures have long valued. Thus the ancient Greeks spoke of the 'Age of Gold' (when life was good); King Midas wished to turn everything he touched into gold; and the Spanish conquerors of South America were driven by a desire to find the mythical City of Gold, which, it was said, was presided over by a chief called El Dorado – the 'Golden One'.

Blood is the substance most closely connected with life, and its meaning is clear: it stands for the life force. The Aztecs regarded blood sacrifice as necessary to sustain the gods, and blood takes on ever richer symbolism in Christianity; at supper the night before his crucifixion, Christ said of the wine, 'This is my blood' – a statement recalled today in the Mass. Similarly, the Book of Exodus describes the Promised Land as 'flowing with milk and honey' – a vision that must have appealed to the Israelites as they struggled in the wilderness, even as God sent miraculous manna to sustain them.

Many substances that have particular significance are remarkably humble. Clay, for example, appears in several creation myths. The Islamic tradition asserts that man is made of clay; and in the Old Testament the long-suffering Job confirms: 'I also am formed out of clay.' Jewish mythology includes tales of the Golem, an avenging creature made out of clay and then animated with a spell. In Aboriginal myth, humans are pulled from the clay or mud.

Metals other than gold were important. Iron features heavily in Aboriginal mythology – specifically in the form of red ochre, which is considered *maban*, or magical. Ochre was valued by the early San peoples of South Africa, who seem to have accorded it life-giving properties. The epic relating the hero Jason's voyages include the story of Talus, a bronze giant who bombarded Jason's ship on Crete; and in the Old Testament, Moses sets up the Brazen Serpent as a sacred object. Later Rabbinic mythologies spoke of the bronze god Moloch, in whose body children were burnt as a sacrifice. Various metals known today take their names from mythological characters, including Plutonium, Uranium and Mercury.

PRECEDING PAGES *The Ocean of Milk is churned to produce the elixir of immortality.* OPPOSITE *Moses descends from Mount Sinai to find the Israelites worshipping a golden calf.* ABOVE *Gold had sacred significance for the Mesoamericans. Here it re-creates a shining solar disc.*

The hardest substance in mythology is adamant, a term that seems to refer to a number of highly resistant materials, from gemstones to metal. In Greek legend Cronus castrated his father Uranus using an adamantine sickle, and Perseus beheaded Medusa using an adamantine blade. Both Prometheus and Loki were said to have been bound with adamantine chains.

Many mythological substances are related to immortality. Alchemists for centuries sought out the Philosopher's Stone, which apart from turning base metals into gold would provide the elixir of life. In Hindu mythology the drink called *soma* fulfils the same role, while in Greek mythology the gods sustain themselves with ambrosia.

The beginnings of life – according to Norse accounts of the universe's origins – depended on two fundamental elements: ice (found in the primordial, freezing world of Niflheim) and fire (from its opposite world, burning Muspelheim), which were separated by a yawning void called Ginnungagap. In Niflheim there was a well or spring, at the bottom of which lived countless writhing serpents. They produced venom that rose to the surface and combined with the ice; once this mixture had fallen into the void, it was vaporized by the fires of Muspelheim. The result was a strange, magical substance called *eitr*. This was the stuff of life, and from it the first giant, Ymir, was formed. As Ymir slept, the sweat from his armpits turned into further giants. He and his offspring were nursed by the cow Audumla, who was also created from *eitr*.

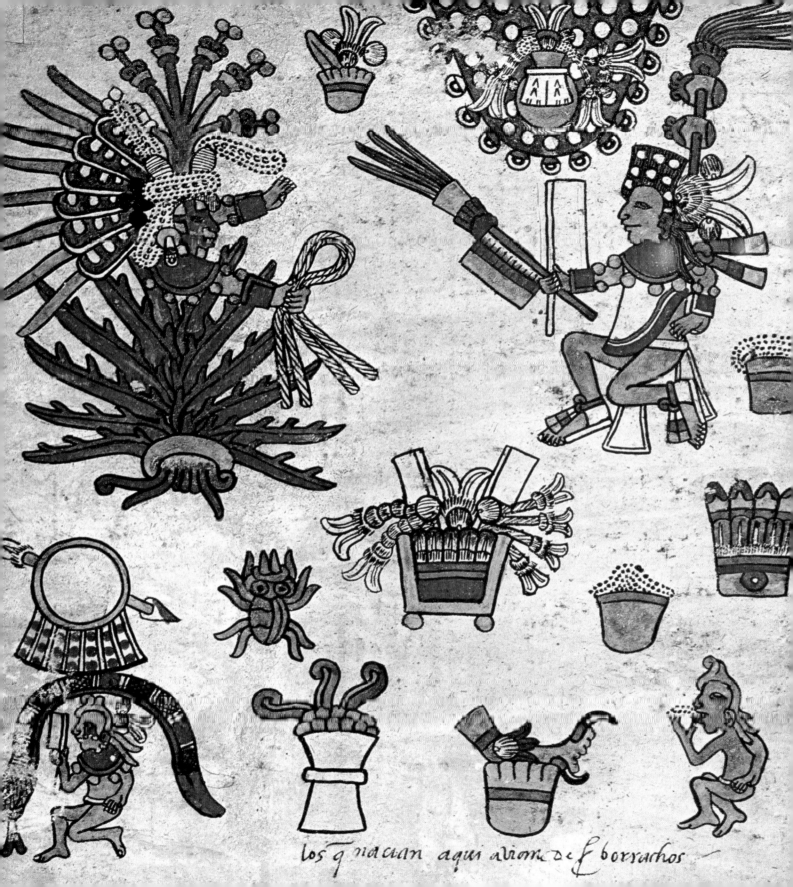

los q̃ nacian aqui alia~ de ẽ borrachos

Gold

||||||||||||||||||||||||||||||||

For the ancient Egyptians, gold was especially valued because of its association with Ra, the sun god. In South America, the legendary Inca chief named El Dorado was said to have a garden in which all of the animals and plants were made of gold.

In Greek legend, the hero Jason is given a quest to find and bring back the Golden Fleece – that is, the pelt of a golden ram that was kept in a sacred grove and guarded by a dragon. Jason killed the monster and returned with the ram's skin. Since then, the Golden Fleece has been interpreted as a symbol of royal authority, a type of gold mining, or even just the wealth that existed on the Greek world's eastern fringes.

Perhaps the most famous myth involving gold is that of Midas. Granted a wish by Bacchus because he had looked after Silenus (who had got drunk and then lost), Midas asked for the power to turn everything he touched into gold. His new gift initially pleased him, but when his food and drink also turned to metal he began to have regrets. Praying to Bacchus to remove what he now saw as a curse, Midas was told to bathe in the waters of the Pactolus – one explanation for why the river contains so much gold.

ABOVE *Jason retrieves the Golden Fleece from a grove sacred to the god Ares.* OPPOSITE *Danaë and her maid wonder at the appearance of a mysterious shower of gold (Zeus in disguise).*

OPPOSITE *The king of the Incas in the eyes of Europeans: El Dorado, the 'Golden One', having gold applied to his body.* ABOVE *Midas begins to realize that not everything need be made of gold.*

Milk

In Hindu mythology the vast Ocean of Milk produces the life-giving elixir *amrita*, and is also where Vishnu floats, asleep on the back of Shesha. Ghee, made from cow's milk, is vital to Hindu ritual.

The Egyptian goddess Hathor often appears in the guise of Hesat, a dairy cow, whose name means 'milk'. She suckled the other gods.

The Milky Way for the Greeks was formed of milk from the breast of Hera. Zeus, who was fond of Heracles and regretted that his son's mother was mortal, decided to get his wife to suckle the child while she was asleep. When she awoke and realized what was happening, she pulled the infant from her breast, and the milk sprayed into the sky.

OPPOSITE *Milk from Hera's breast sprays into the sky, forming the Milky Way.* BELOW *A statue of the Virgin Mary nursing her son, of a type known as the 'Virgo Lactans'.* RIGHT *The goddess Hathor breastfeeding.*

Blood

||||||||||||||||||||||||||||||||||||

Blood has special significance in many mythologies. The Aztecs believed that a constant supply of blood was necessary for the survival of the gods, especially the sun god Tonatiuh. Blood sacrifices can also be found in Norse mythology and rituals.

In Christianity, too, blood is connected to a type of sacrifice – that represented by Christ's crucifixion. Especially in the art of the Middle Ages, his blood was shown being caught in a chalice, to highlight a connection with the Mass.

The life-giving properties of blood appear again in Hindu mythology. When Durga wounded the demon Raktavija, she was dismayed to see that every drop of his spilt blood generated a clone of her enemy. Her solution to this problem was somewhat gruesome: the goddess Kali went around the battlefield licking up every drop, before sucking all of the blood out of Raktavija.

In Greek myth, the blood of the gods was known as *ichor*, and thought to be golden in colour. It was highly poisonous to humans. For the hero Siegfried (see p. 308), however, bathing in the blood of a dragon made him invincible.

OPPOSITE ABOVE *A blood sacrifice is offered to an Aztec deity.* OPPOSITE BELOW *Medea drains Jason's blood in order to rejuvenate him.* RIGHT *A Tibetan chart indicating good and bad times for bloodletting, and when to guard against demons.*

UT LOTH SALVETUR NE RESPICIAT PROHIBETUR

SIC VIGANTRE · VEHI PER HEROD IS REGNA SABEI

Salt

Salt is necessary for life, but in Norse mythology it is the very stuff of life, since the cow Audumla licked one of the first beings out of a block of salt.

According to the Old Testament Book of Genesis, Lot and his wife fled the city of Sodom ahead of its destruction. Like Orpheus, they were told not to look back. Lot's wife gave one backward glance, however, and was turned into a pillar of salt.

The Aztec salt goddess is Huixtocihuatl, the sister of Tlaloc, while the Romans recognized a seawater goddess called Salacia. Salt appears frequently as an offering to the gods in various mythologies.

One myth, as told in the old Norse poem *Grottasöngr*, involved two giantesses called Menia and Fenia. The sea king forced them to turn a millstone and grind salt, but the whole contraption fell into the sea, turning the water salty.

ABOVE *Lot's wife turns to face the city of Sodom – and is transformed into a pillar of salt.* OPPOSITE *The giantesses Menia and Fenia are forced to mill salt.*

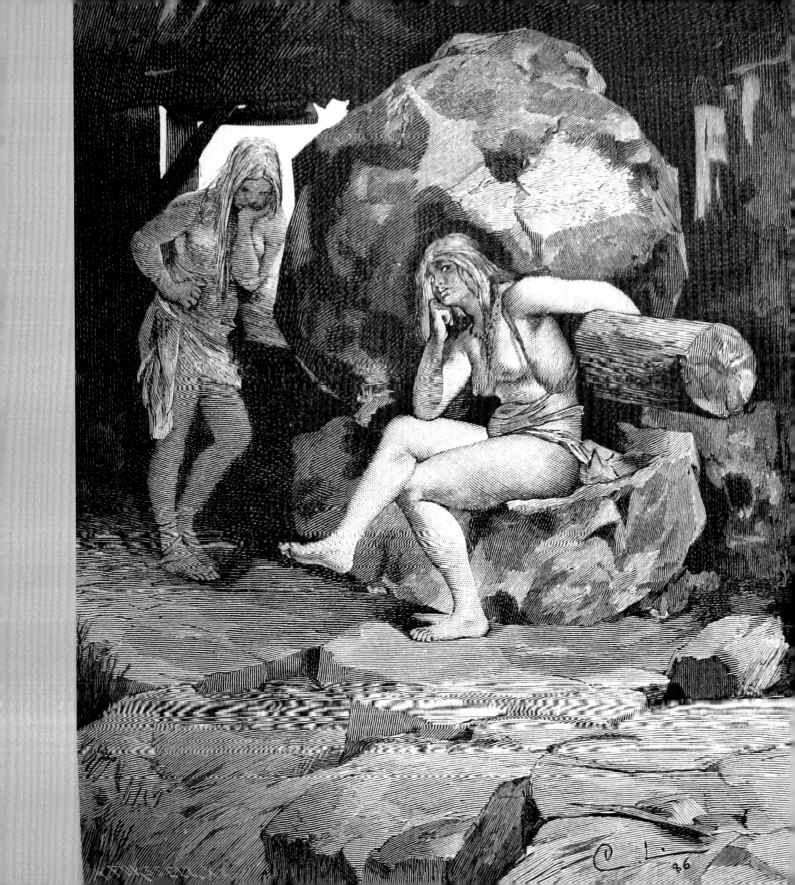

Alcohol

Disembarking from the Ark, Noah planted a vineyard, produced wine and proceeded to get drunk. One of his sons, Ham, saw him naked and inebriated, and was cursed as a result. A later episode in the Old Testament describes how Lot's daughters got their father drunk in order to have children by him.

In Aztec culture the alcoholic drink called *pulque* played an important role. It was made from agave, and its origins were supposedly divine: it was sent by Quetzalcoatl to encourage humans to dance and sing. *Pulque* was also given to those about to be sacrificed.

In Greek mythology the champion of alcohol was Dionysus (known to the Romans as Bacchus). He was the god of wine and the unfettered enjoyment of alcohol. His friend the aged Silenus represented the downside of drinking, and was often shown drunk or asleep.

In Hindu mythology the creator of alcohol is the *asura* Varuni, the consort of Varuna. For the ancient Egyptians, the lion goddess Sekhmet was sent by the gods to devour humanity. She was stopped in her massacre when a huge vat of beer was dyed red. She drank it, thinking it was blood, and become so inebriated that the carnage ceased.

OPPOSITE *The appallingly drunk Silenus, who is wreathed in vines and bears grapes.* BELOW *Odysseus and his companions blind the Cyclops Polyphemus, having given him lots of strong wine.*

Apples

Apples crop up frequently in myths, and are almost always associated with life or knowledge. In the Bible, Eve famously persuaded Adam to eat the forbidden fruit of the Tree of Knowledge; it has traditionally been depicted as an apple, though the Bible is not so specific.

In the Greek legend of Atalanta, who was determined not to take a husband, this wild princess eventually promised to marry whichever of her suitors could beat her in a race. Since she was particularly fast, Atalanta felt that she was in no danger, but when Hippomenes agreed to the challenge Aphrodite gave him three golden apples to distract her. He dropped them at intervals, and Atalanta could not help but stop to pick them up, and so lost the race.

The myth known as the Judgment of Paris also includes a golden apple, tossed by Eris ('Discord') at the goddesses Aphrodite, Hera and Athena, in order to provoke an argument. In Norse mythology golden apples give eternal life and are the source of the gods' powers.

BELOW *In the Book of Genesis, an apple spelt the downfall of humankind.* OPPOSITE *The three goddesses approach the sleeping Paris to request his judgment; Mercury holds the golden apple that prompted their rivalry.*

mercure venus juno pallas

Paris

Comment paris expofa au
Roy priam fon fonge Et

Dont me vint en
auifion que pre
fent moy eftoit

la vifion et promineffe de
la Deeffe Venus

a iuge pour en determiner
felon ce que tu verras leur
Droit elre apparaiſant par

THE TREE OF DEATH.

But a corrupt tree bringeth forth evil fruit. St Mat VII. 17   Cut it down, why cumbereth it the ground ? St Luke XII. 7

OPPOSITE *In the Christian tradition, the apple symbolizes original sin, and therefore death. This diagram extends the metaphor, giving each apple a literal transgression.* ABOVE *Atalanta stops to pick up the golden apples, and thereby loses her race with Hippomenes.*

Honey

|||||||||||||||||||||||||||||||||||||||

For the ancient Greeks, honey was closely associated with the gods and symbolized knowledge. It was said that the hero Achilles was fed on honey as a child, giving him great eloquence.

The Old Testament is full of references to honey, suggestive of sweetness and leisure, and one of the chapters of the Koran, entitled 'The Bee', describes it as a 'cure for men'. In Hinduism, honey is used in worship, or as a sacrifice. There is also a tale that, when the Buddha went on retreat, a monkey brought him honey to sustain him.

The Maya, too, believed honey to be a divine food. They had a god, Ah-Muzen-Cab, specifically dedicated to beekeeping and honey.

BELOW *Bacchus (right foreground) discovers honey – a step on the long road to civilization.* OPPOSITE *Cupid realizes that, to obtain sweet honey, one has to endure the stings of bees – a little like the experience of being in love.*

7

HEROES
||||||||||||||||||||||||||||

The figure of the hero or heroine is central to all mythologies. Sometimes human, sometimes divine, heroes battle against monsters and engage in perilous adventures; the struggle and danger are essential to the story, and most heroes finish their adventures wiser. According to the ancient Greeks, the Heroic Age was the fourth stage of human existence, after the ages of gold, silver and bronze. These mighty characters served to overcome any elements of chaos that remained from an older time; a classic example of this clash of systems is the Anglo-Saxon *Beowulf* epic, in which the hero relentlessly fights the evil monster Grendel, Grendel's mother and a dragon.

This is not to say that all heroes are like Beowulf, Heracles or Thor, wielding swords, clubs and axes, and engaged in constant warfare. Many important figures, such as Jesus Christ and the Buddha, are heroes in the sense that they challenge the orthodoxy and overcome temptation. Other heroes liberate their people not from monsters, but from slavery, as did Moses.

The scholar Joseph Campbell identified the key elements of the hero story, which he labelled as 'departure' (the call to adventure; supernatural aid; crossing the first threshold), 'initiation' (the road of trials; woman as temptress; atonement with the father) and 'return' (magic flight; rescue from without; the crossing of the return threshold; master of two worlds). This pattern, Campbell claimed, could be found in the lives of Jesus Christ, the Buddha and Moses, among other significant figures.

Hero stories can indeed seem formulaic. For example, heroes typically have unusual births or a divine parent. Heracles was the son of Zeus, and Jesus was born to a virgin. Gilgamesh was described as two-thirds divine, since his mother was a goddess and his father semi-mortal. The principal figure of the Finnish *Kalevala* saga, Väinämöinen, was originally a god, but his role changed over the years into that of a hero.

Often heroes face their first danger at a young age. Moses was abandoned in the Nile to avoid being massacred by Pharaoh; Christ fled to Egypt to avoid being murdered by Herod; and Heracles was threatened by two snakes sent to kill him by Hera (he throttled them). The Persian hero Rostam, while still a young boy, killed a rampaging white elephant. Gilgamesh – as later versions of the story tell us – was thrown from a tower as a baby, but was saved and raised by a farmer. Siegfried was found and raised by a blacksmith. In Theseus' case, his absent father left his sandals and sword under a rock; only when Theseus was strong enough to lift the rock would he be ready to begin his journey.

PRECEDING PAGES *The Persian hero Rostam kills the White Demon – the last of his seven labours.* OPPOSITE *The heroic Cadmus kills the dragon with his spear.* ABOVE LEFT *Heracles pursuing Geras ('Old Age')* ABOVE *The Japanese hero Kintaro, raised by a mountain hag.*

Hero figures are also precocious. Christ discussed religion with the elders in the temple at the age of twelve. Achilles was taught by the wise centaur Chiron, as were Jason, Ajax, and possibly even Heracles. Heracles apparently did not excel in music, since he killed his tutor, Linus, after being told off for his mistakes.

Heracles' strength was another hallmark of heroes, who were often called upon to demonstrate what sets them apart. Rama strung the mighty bow of Shiva, and the young Arthur removed the sword stuck fast in the stone. Rostam performed seven impossible tasks; Heracles, on the other hand, was originally obliged to carry out ten tasks, but he was said to have completed two with help, and in the end had to perform twelve. Sometimes the hero's strength is mental, as was the case with Christ when he was asked to sacrifice himself.

Some heroes had accomplices. Gilgamesh, for instance, was accompanied by the strange, uncouth, wild Enkidu, who became as a brother to the hero. Heracles was aided by his nephew Iolaus, especially in defeating the Hydra (as Heracles cut off the heads, Iolaus cauterized the necks).

Heroes were accessible in a way that gods were not. For the Greeks, Heracles and Perseus had unquestionably existed; and even Alexander the Great claimed descent from the less-than-historical Achilles. Moses, too, was a real historical figure for later Jews, Christians and Muslims. Some believe King Arthur to have been an early defender of the British Isles against Saxon invaders. Gilgamesh, a real king of the Sumerian city of Uruk in the third millennium BC, is remembered in Mesopotamian mythology as a demigod, responsible for building the city's unbreachable walls. In the same way Theseus is associated with Athens' foundation.

Heroes did not always act honourably. Rama treated his wife with undue suspicion (and came to regret it); Theseus deserted Ariadne on an island; Heracles killed his wife and children in a fit of madness; and Jason abandoned Medea in favour of a princess. Jason's sad end – killed by a piece of the *Argo*, which fell on him as he slept under the stern – tells us that ultimately heroes were often subject to the same misfortunes as humans.

OPPOSITE *An Ethiopian depiction of St George killing the dragon that had terrorized a city.* ABOVE *Achilles taught how to use a bow and arrow by the wise centaur Chiron.*

Miraculous Births

||||||||||||||||||||||||||||||||||||||||||||||||||||||||||||||||||||||||||||||||||||||||||||||||||||||||||||||||||||

Many heroes have divine parentage. Theseus was supposedly fathered by Poseidon and Aegeus (who both slept with his mother during the course of one night), and Heracles' father was Zeus. Other significant conceptions were heralded by portents. When the Buddha was conceived, his mother had a dream of a white elephant; and his birth under a tree prefigured his later meditation under the sacred fig.

The Persian god Mithras was supposedly born from a rock, and the Persian equivalent of Heracles, Rostam, was born by caesarean section after he would not stop growing in his mother's womb.

Christ's conception was announced by the archangel Gabriel, who appeared to Mary, and yet the birth of the world's saviour was extremely humble, taking place in a stable. His earthly father, Joseph, was descended from King David, providing a link to an earlier heroic figure.

LEFT *The Persian god Mithras – worhsipped throughout the Roman empire – was said to have been born from a rock.* ABOVE *According to some versions of the myth, Poseidon sired Theseus.* OPPOSITE *Despite being the son of God, Jesus was born in a stable.* FOLLOWING PAGES *(left) The Buddha's mother, a queen, gives birth under a sal tree. (right) Rostam was born by caesarian section – a highly unusual event that distinguished him from other mortals.*

Monstrous Foes

||||||||||||||||||||||||||||||||||||||||||||||||||||||||||||||||||||||||||||||||||||||||||||||||||||||||

Monsters are central to heroic tales, representing the forces of chaos that the hero must overcome in order to restore law and order. That they stand for chaos is evident from their physical appearance, since almost all are composites of other creatures.

The most impressive monsters are perhaps dragons. Jason, Perseus, Thor, Cadmus, St George and Heracles were all obliged to fight dragons or dragon-type creatures, either to complete their quests or to rid the world of evil. Others had more peculiar foes: Theseus battled against the Minotaur, while Gilgamesh faced scorpion people. Another of Gilgamesh's adversaries was Humbaba, whose face resembled that of a lion, but was made of a single coil, like intestines.

Demons appear almost as often. Japanese demons – known as *oni* – patrol hell with iron clubs, just as their Christian counterparts punish the damned. The biblical Book of Revelation predicts a colossal, final battle between the Devil – in the form of a monstrous beast – and St Michael. The Hindu goddesses Durga and Kali battle against such demons as Mahishasura.

Monsters can also represent the 'other', the unknown; and the greatest unknown, even today, is the seas. Odysseus had to avoid the six-headed Scylla, who guarded passage through a narrow strait, while the Bible describes perhaps the greatest sea monster of all, Leviathan.

OPPOSITE *(clockwise, from top left) A harpy, a giant, a griffin and a faun. In the centre is the fire-breathing Chimera, composed of a lion with a goat's head on its back.* ABOVE *One of Cadmus' followers is devoured by a fierce dragon.*

OPPOSITE *Giants and dwarfs are both important figures in Norse mythology.* RIGHT *Blake's illustration of the 'Great Red Dragon' from the Book of Revelation.*

Perseus

||||||||||||||||||||||||||||||||||||||||||||||||||||||||||||

Perseus was one of ancient Greece's earliest heroes. The son of Zeus and Danaë (see p. 258), he and his mother were locked in a trunk and cast into the sea by Danaë's father, Acrisius, who had heard that his son would kill him. They washed up on the island of Seriphos, where Perseus was raised by the fisherman Dictys.

Perseus was sent to bring back the head of the snake-haired Gorgon Medusa. This most hideous of creatures had a face that could turn creatures to stone. With the aid of Athena and the Hesperides, Perseus acquired a sickle and an invisibility helmet (from Poseidon); guided by the reflection of his shield, he was able to cut off Medusa's head.

From Medusa's blood sprang the winged horse Pegasus, who helped Perseus on his next challenge: the rescue of Andromeda. This princess had been left by her father as an offering for a sea monster. Perseus killed the beast (possibly using the Gorgon's head), and then rescued and married Andromeda – giving Medusa's head to Athena, who mounted it on her shield. Perseus became king of Mycenae, founding a lineage that eventually led to Heracles.

LEFT AND OPPOSITE *Perseus holds up the horrific head of the Gorgon Medusa, which could turn those who looked at it to stone.*

BELOW *Perseus rescues Andromeda from the terrible sea monster.* BELOW RIGHT *The mother of Perseus was Danaë – seduced by Zeus, who was disguised as a shower of gold.*

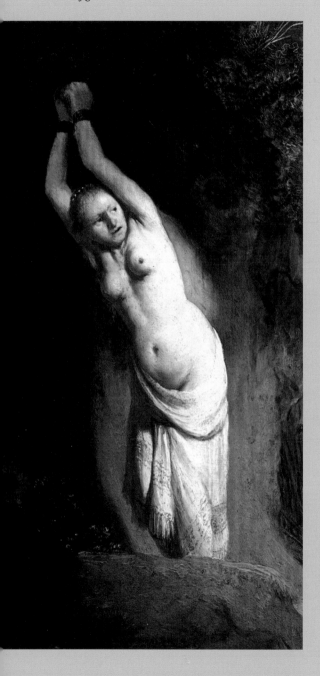

In some versions of the story, Perseus rides on the winged horse Pegasus to defeat the sea monster.

Theseus

Since both slept with his mother during the night she conceived, Theseus' father was either Aegeus, king of Athens, or Poseidon disguised as Aegeus. Either way, Aegeus left his sandals and sword hidden under a stone, so that when the boy was old enough to lift it, he could go and find his father.

On the road to Athens, Theseus encountered several murderers and bandits. One of them, Procrustes, would stretch or cut down guests to fit his iron bed; Sinis would tear people in half using pine trees; and Sciron made his victims wash his feet before kicking them off a cliff. Theseus destroyed each of them using their own methods. Though Aegeus did not recognize Theseus when he arrived in Athens, his wife, Medea, did, and tried to poison him.

The best-known story involving Theseus is that of the Minotaur. Each year, Athens paid Crete a tribute of seven boys

and seven girls, who were fed to the half-human, half-bull Minotaur. Theseus volunteered to be among them, but on his arrival in Crete King Minos's daughter, Ariadne, fell in love with him, and gave him a ball of string to help him escape the labyrinth in which the Minotaur lived. Theseus killed the monster and then escaped with Ariadne. The tale ends in tragedy, however: as he was travelling home, Theseus in his excitement forgot to change the colour of his ship's sail from black to white; Aegeus, reading the black as a sign of his son's death, threw himself into the sea henceforth known as the Aegean.

ABOVE *The deeds of Theseus. In the centre, Theseus carries the dead Minotaur out of the labyrinth; around the edge, we see Theseus with Sinis, the Crommyonian Sow, Cercyon, Procrustes and Sciron.*
OPPOSITE *Theseus lifts the stone to find his father's sandals and sword.*

Heracles

Heracles (known to the Romans as Hercules) is the archetypal hero, and a role model to generations of Greek and Roman men. The son of Zeus and Alcmene – and therefore semi-mortal – he was endowed with superhuman strength. At times peaceful, he could also fly into rages – as when he murdered his music teacher, and his first wife and children.

Heracles is best known for completing the twelve impossible labours set him by King Eurystheus (possibly as penance for murdering his family). Some tasks involved killing ferocious, supernatural creatures, including the Nemean Lion, the Lernaean Hydra and the brazen-beaked Stymphalian Birds, while in other cases he had to bring back the creatures alive, as happened with the Ceryneian Hind, the Erymanthian Boar, the Cretan Bull, and Cerberus, the guardian of Hades. In other labours Heracles was required to gather animals (the Mares of Diomedes and the Cattle of Geryon), clean the filthy Augean Stables, steal the Girdle of Hippolyta and gather the Apples of the Hesperides.

Some of these tasks Heracles achieved through brute strength, but he was also crafty. For example, he cleaned the stables by diverting a nearby river through them. And he persuaded Atlas to retrieve the Apples of the Hesperides for him, while Heracles supported the skies.

Heracles' adventures did not end there. Other myths describe how he joined Jason's Argonauts, shot and killed the eagle tormenting Prometheus, and strangled the giant Antaeus.

Heracles' death came from an unexpected quarter. In an earlier episode he had shot the centaur Nessus with an arrow dipped in the Hydra's poisonous blood. As Nessus died, he told Heracles' wife that his blood could be used to ensure that Heracles remained faithful. Much later, she gave Heracles a shirt tainted with Nessus' blood, which poisoned him. With his remaining strength, Heracles built his own funeral pyre; once his mortal part had died, he ascended to Olympus.

OPPOSITE *Heracles kills the terrible, flesh-eating Cacus, son of Hephaestus.* ABOVE RIGHT *The infant Heracles strangles a snake.* BELOW *Heracles with (from left to right) the Nemean Lion, the Lernaean Hydra, the Erymanthian Boar, the Ceryneian Hind, the Stymphalian Birds, the Girdle of Hippolyta, the Augean Stables, the Cretan Bull and the Mares of Diomedes.*

OPPOSITE *Heracles wrestles with the sea god Triton, son of Poseidon.*
ABOVE *Heracles with his third wife, Deianira. On the floor lies the dead centaur Nessus, whose trickery would lead to the hero's death.*

King Arthur

The historicity of the figure we know as King Arthur is unproved, though some scholars believe that he was possibly a Romano-British leader defending the British Isles against Saxon invaders. Most of the classic tales of Arthurian mythology – Camelot, Merlin, the Lady in the Lake and the Holy Grail – were first written down only in the 12th century.

According to these accounts, Arthur's father was Uther Pendragon, who had seduced his enemy's wife while in disguise. Uther died without a legitimate heir, but Arthur proved his right to the throne when he alone was able to take the sword from the stone in which it was lodged.

In his castle, Camelot, King Arthur gathered about him exceptional knights such as Gawain and Lancelot. They sat at the famous Round Table, a symbol of their equality.

Arthur's final battle was with Mordred, who had married Arthur's wife in the king's absence. It took place at a spot named Camlann, and led to the deaths of both combatants.

ABOVE *Arthur being crowned (left), and the king with one of his knights.* OPPOSITE *This 15th-century depiction shows Arthur returning to his beloved Camelot.*

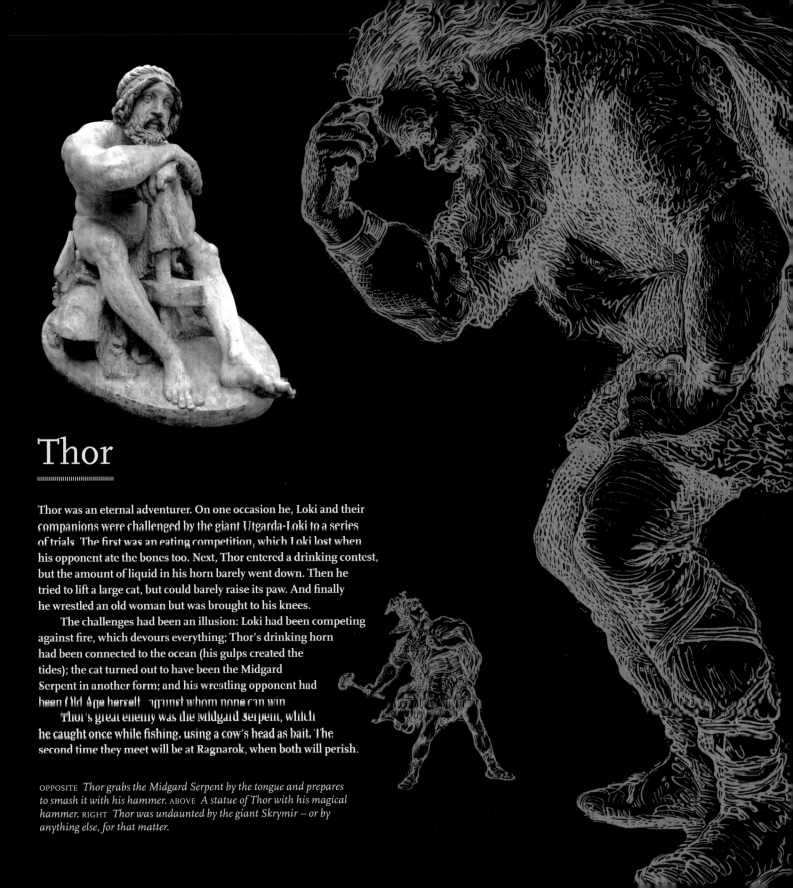

Thor

Thor was an eternal adventurer. On one occasion he, Loki and their companions were challenged by the giant Utgarda-Loki to a series of trials. The first was an eating competition, which Loki lost when his opponent ate the bones too. Next, Thor entered a drinking contest, but the amount of liquid in his horn barely went down. Then he tried to lift a large cat, but could barely raise its paw. And finally he wrestled an old woman but was brought to his knees.

The challenges had been an illusion: Loki had been competing against fire, which devours everything; Thor's drinking horn had been connected to the ocean (his gulps created the tides); the cat turned out to have been the Midgard Serpent in another form; and his wrestling opponent had been Old Age herself, against whom none can win.

Thor's great enemy was the Midgard Serpent, which he caught once while fishing, using a cow's head as bait. The second time they meet will be at Ragnarok, when both will perish.

OPPOSITE *Thor grabs the Midgard Serpent by the tongue and prepares to smash it with his hammer.* ABOVE *A statue of Thor with his magical hammer.* RIGHT *Thor was undaunted by the giant Skrymir – or by anything else, for that matter.*

Gilgamesh

Gilgamesh appears in the world's oldest epic, dating to over 3,500 years ago. He is described as coming from the city of Uruk, and was probably based on a real king.

As the epic relates, Gilgamesh was a brave warrior, but his womanizing caused the gods to send him a companion, the animal-like Enkidu. The pair's first challenge is to kill Humbaba, the monster guarding Enlil's sacred Cedar Forest. Gilgamesh then upsets the goddess Inanna (Ishtar) by refusing her advances, so she sends the mighty Bull of Heaven – which Gilgamesh also slaughters. In retaliation, the gods kill Enkidu. Gilgamesh, devastated, descends into the underworld to overcome death. He passes the two scorpion-people who guard the entrance, and meets Siduri, who helps him cross the river of the underworld. There, Gilgamesh meets Utnapishtim, the survivor of the flood (see p. 306).

Gilgamesh asks him the secret of eternal life. However, when he is challenged to stay awake for six nights, Gilgamesh fails, and realizes that he is mortal. Nonetheless, Utnapishtim informs him of a plant that maintains youth. Gilgamesh retrieves it, but it is stolen by snakes (explaining why those animals shed their skins). Finally accepting his mortality, he returns to Uruk.

LEFT *The face of one of Gilgamesh's adversaries, Humbaba, said to resemble coiled intestines.* OPPOSITE *Gilgamesh appears between two bull-men, who support a winged sun disk.*

Sigmund
and Siegfried

Sigmund and Siegfried, father and son, are the greatest heroes in Germanic and Norse mythology. Both feature prominently in the 13th-century *Volsunga Saga* and in the epic *Nibelungenlied*, both of which in turn inspired Wagner's celebrated opera cycle *The Ring of the Nibelung*.

Sigmund, a descendent of Odin, proved his lineage by removing the sword Gram from a tree. This sword was later shattered when Sigmund mistakenly attacked Odin, and the pieces were safeguarded for Siegfried (in Norse, Sigurd).

One of the most significant legends connected with Siegfried involves his foster father, Regin, and Regin's brother, Fafnir. After inheriting cursed treasure, Fafnir turns himself into a dragon. Siegfried resolves to kill the dragon, and Odin advises him to dig a trench to catch the blood.

Siegfried slays the dragon using Gram and bathes in Fafnir's blood, to make himself invincible. After drinking some of it, he finds that he can understand the birds, from which he learns that Regin intends to kill him. He kills Regin first, then eats the dragon's heart, which gives him the gift of prophecy.

RIGHT *Siegfried slays the dragon Fafnir.* OPPOSITE *Sigurd (Siegfried), on the left, tests the newly repaired sword – and breaks it.*

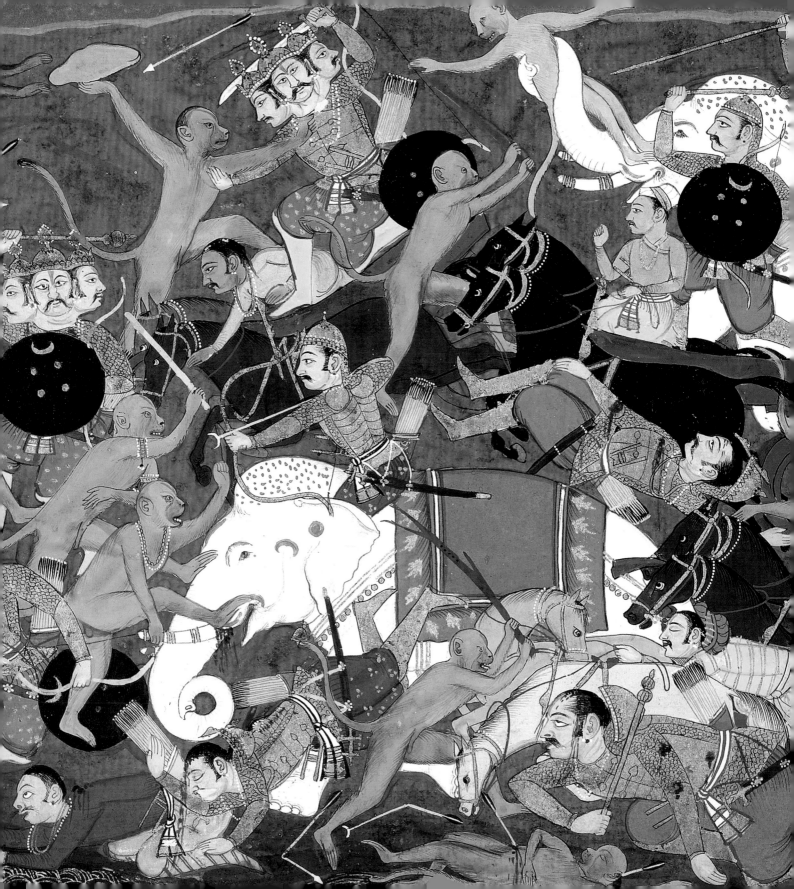

8

QUESTS,
JOURNEYS
AND EPICS

Mythological epics have a long history, stretching back to the *Epic of Gilgamesh*, first written down at the end of the 3rd millennium BC. Since then many different cultures have produced their own sagas, including the *Iliad* and the *Odyssey*, the *Ramayana*, the *Mahabharata*, the *Prose Edda* and *Poetic Edda*, *Beowulf* and the *Kalevala* – all of which are mainstays of mythology, as well as being key sources of information on gods, goddesses and even everyday life. In some cases these texts are overtly religious, but more often they simply tell stories.

Some epics can be associated with founding myths and concepts of nationhood. The story of the Hebrews' Exodus from Egypt, as told in the Old Testament, and their subsequent wanderings in the desert are connected with the origins of Israel. In the 19th century, local folk tales and native mythologies were gathered together into the book known as the *Kalevala*, which helped give the Finnish nation a sense of identity. The *Nibelungenlied* cycle was fundamental to Germanic culture. The *Aeneid*, which relates the fate of the Trojan hero Aeneas after the fall of Troy (and which was written by the Roman poet Virgil in the 1st century BC), essentially offers an explanation of Rome's founding and the origins of its people.

Some of these epics involve quests for a particular object or power – particularly the secret of eternal life or spiritual enlightenment, as is the case with the quest for Holy Grail. The Chinese epic novel *Journey to the West* documents a search for key Buddhist texts in India, while in Greek myth Jason travelled in search of the Golden Fleece.

The *Mahabharata* – one of the great Sanskrit epics – tells of the feud between two families, the Pandavas and the Kauravas. The world's longest epic poem, it probably appeared in its final form in the 4th century AD. Just as in the *Iliad*, the Greek gods were related to characters fighting on both sides, were partisan, and occasionally switched allegiances. In the Trojan War, gods such

PRECEDING PAGES *The battle between the armies of Rama and the King of Lanka.* OPPOSITE *The story of Jason, who was commanded to bring back the Golden Fleece.* ABOVE *Achilles fights the Amazon queen Penthesilea.*

as Poseidon would temporarily take to the battlefield themselves before being ordered off by Zeus.

Magic often introduces a note of chance to mythological quests. Circe and Medea both helped and hindered Greek heroes with their spells; and Japanese, Chinese and Irish mythologies all mention time travel. Ovid's *Metamorphoses* is a catalogue of magical transformations, of sudden appearances and disappearances (see p. 248).

The protagonists of quests and epics are almost always male, though women can play a decisive role. The Trojan War was sparked off by Paris's infatuation with Helen, and Odysseus is constantly waylaid by temptresses. Rama is in pursuit of his abducted wife: when he finds her, she has to throw herself onto a pyre to convince him that she has not been unfaithful. The characters in *Journey to the West* pass through a land ruled by women – in the author's mind clearly an inversion of the natural order – and Heracles fights against the female Amazons. Jason and his Argonauts arrive at the island of Lemnos to find that the women have killed their husbands.

The islands that Odysseus discovers on his ten-year wanderings reflect the 'otherness' of foreign countries at a time when long-distance travel was far less common. Just as Pliny later described the 'monstrous races' to be found in places such as India and Ethiopia, epic journeys offered an opportunity for flights of fancy. In *Journey to the West*, for example, the four heroes pass through strange countries and have to adapt themselves to peculiar customs, to fit in.

Perhaps the ultimate destination, however, was the underworld. Several heroes travelled there, including Orpheus, Gilgamesh, the Maya Hero Twins, and Christ. Each has returned to the land of the living with some new knowledge or gift, and a few even managed to conquer death itself.

ABOVE *The most dramatic moment in the biblical Book of Exodus: the waters of the Red Sea wipe out Pharaoh's men.* OPPOSITE *Oedipus appears before the Sphinx, pondering its riddle – though staring the monster directly in the eye.*

Magical Weapons

Magical weapons are essential for heroes embarking on a quest. King Arthur wielded Excalibur, forged on the island of Avalon and given to him by the Lady in the Lake; and the Germanic hero Sigmund drew a sword from a tree.

The Monkey King in *Journey to the West* carries a magical iron rod that can change size. Obtained from the Dragon King of the Eastern Sea, it weighs several tons, but can be kept behind Monkey's ear. Thor's hammer, Mjölnir – which created thunder and was able to destroy mountains – could also be miniaturized. Odin's weapon of choice was the spear Gungnir: fashioned by dwarves, it always hit its quarry. The Japanese Susanoo, god of the sea and of storms, discovered the sword called Kusanagi in a beast's tail and used it to control the wind.

ABOVE *An amulet in the form of Thor's hammer, Mjölnir.* RIGHT *In* Journey to the West *Monkey always travels with his magical iron bar.* OPPOSITE *The Lady in the Lake receives Arthur's sword, Excalibur, as the king sits dying on the shore.*

vant gyfles voit que
faire li couient· fire

Jason

The greatest myths involving Jason begin with his visit to King Pelias, in Iolcus, Thessaly. The king had been warned to beware of a man with only one shoe – and Jason had lost a shoe in a stream during his journey. Pelias decided to send Jason on a long, dangerous quest, commissioning him to bring back the Golden Fleece.

Jason assembled a band of men to sail in the magical boat called the *Argo* (from which they were called 'Argonauts'), including Heracles and the twins Castor and Pollux. The Argonauts' itinerary took in an island populated only by women, some thieving harpies, and cliffs that crushed all passing ships. Eventually they arrived in Colchis, in modern-day Georgia, where the king, Aeëtes, agreed to give the fleece to Jason if he could complete three tasks. The first was to plough a field using fire-breathing oxen; the second, to sow some dragon's teeth that grew into hostile soldiers (Jason contrived to make them kill each other); and the third, to overcome the dragon that guarded the Golden Fleece (Aeëtes' daughter, the sorceress Medea – who had fallen in love with Jason – gave him a potion to make the dragon sleep).

Returning home with Medea, Jason met another enchantress, Circe, and passed the Sirens. Sailing past Crete, they were attacked by an enormous bronze man (Medea made him bleed to death).

In later years Jason decided to marry another woman. Medea was enraged: she killed Jason's wife and his children, and left Jason alone. The hero was killed when a piece of the now-rotten *Argo* fell on his head.

ABOVE *Jason, accompanied by Medea and the Argonauts, takes down the Golden Fleece.* OPPOSITE *Jason and his followers aboard the* Argo.

The Trojan War

Our knowledge of the Trojan War, in which an army of Greeks laid siege to the city of Troy (in modern-day Turkey), comes from a variety of sources, most important of which is Homer's *Iliad*, written in the 8th century BC.

The conflict begins with Paris, the youngest son of Priam, king of Troy. Having decided that Aphrodite is the most beautiful of the goddesses (see p. 270), Paris is awarded the hand of the beautiful Helen (who is already the wife of Menelaus, king of Sparta) and takes her back to Troy.

Discovering Helen's abduction, Menelaus rallies the other kings of Greece (including Odysseus), who had sworn to help each other. They in turn enlist the invulnerable and ruthless Achilles. The Greeks set up camp on the beach close to Troy, and thus begin an exhausting ten-year siege of the city.

Tensions emerge in the Greek camp, and Achilles decides to go home. However, following the death of his companion Patroclus at the hands of Trojan prince Hector he resolves to stay long enough to take revenge.

One day, the Trojans discover that the Greek ships have departed, and that an enormous wooden horse has been left outside the city gates. The Trojans take this to be an offering and drag it into Troy, unaware that it contains Greek soldiers. That night the soldiers leave the horse, open the gates of Troy, and the city falls. However, in the fighting that follows, Achilles is hit by an arrow in his heel – the only part of him that is vulnerable – and dies. Helen returns with Menelaus and is eventually forgiven. Gradually the other survivors of the war make their way home; for Odysseus, the journey takes another ten years.

ABOVE *A relief from the ancient kingdom of Gandhara that almost certainly shows the Trojan Horse being dragged into Troy.* OPPOSITE *The Trojan Aeneas flees with his family as Troy falls to the Greeks.*

ABOVE LEFT AND ABOVE *The Trojan War is perhaps Greek mythology's central story – and continued to capture imaginations in the Middle Ages. These manuscripts show the siege and fall of Troy.* OPPOSITE *The long, drawn-out siege left the men with time on their hands. Here Ajax and Achilles play a game of dice.*

OPPOSITE *Achilles' mother, the sea goddess Thetis, comforts her son after the death of Patroclus.* ABOVE *Achilles, forced to hand over the slave girl Briseis to Agamemnon, reacts with fury and withdraws from the fighting.*

Odysseus

Homer's epic poem the *Odyssey* begins ten years after the fall of Troy. It describes Odysseus' long and eventful journey back to his home on Ithaca, and to his beloved wife, Penelope.

Soon after Odysseus and his men set sail, their ships are blown off course and land on the shores of the Lotus-Eaters. There, two of Odysseus' men eat a substance that makes them forget their homeland. In another episode, Odysseus is captured by the one-eyed Cyclops Polyphemus. The hero blinds him and escapes (see p. 269), but earns the wrath of Polyphemus' father, Poseidon, who curses Odysseus to spend ten years at sea.

Next the men land on the island of Aeolus, the wind god, who gives Odysseus a bag of winds to help him return home, but his companions open it, blowing them off course once more.

On subsequent islands they encounter the cannibalistic, giant Laestrygonians (who capture all but one of Odysseus' ships) and the witch Circe (who turns some of the men into animals). Reaching the western edge of the world, Odysseus

communes with his dead mother, then sails past the Sirens (lashed to the mast, so that he can hear their song in safety), the monstrous Scylla and the whirlpool Charybdis. During a brief stay on the island of Thrinacia, the men eat the sacred cattle of Helios. Cursed once more, all but Odysseus die in a shipwreck soon after.

Odysseus lands on the island of the nymph Calypso, who keeps him captive for seven years, until Hermes persuades her to allow him to leave. Building a raft, Odysseus departs for home. Arriving back in Ithaca, he discovers his house overrun with suitors intent on marrying Penelope. Disguised as a beggar, he seizes his old bow and slaughters the suitors. After twenty years away, he is finally home.

BELOW *One of the most famous scenes from the* Odyssey: *Odysseus sails past the Sirens, lashed to his ship's mast.* OPPOSITE *The wily Odysseus gives wine to the Cyclops Polyphemus (here shown with three eyes instead of the usual one).*

LEFT *Odysseus' voyage took him to the underworld, where he met the prophet Tiresias.*
OPPOSITE *The sorceress Circe turns Odysseus' companions into animals.*

ABOVE *Odysseus with the sorceress Circe.* BELOW *Odysseus meets the young princess Nausicaa.* OPPOSITE *The faithful Penelope at work on her loom, approached by suitors. Through the window we can see Odysseus arriving.*

Exodus

Perhaps the most decisive moment in Jewish mythology is the Israelites' exile from Egypt. They had first gone there in the time of Jacob and Joseph, to flee the famine in Canaan. Four generations later, Pharaoh was worried about the growing Hebrew population and so ordered the death of all Hebrew babies. The infant Moses was left in a basket on the Nile, but was found by Pharaoh's daughter and raised in the royal family. After killing a slave master, he escaped into the desert where God revealed his destiny, speaking through the Burning Bush.

Pharaoh refused to release the Israelites from slavery, so God sent the Ten Plagues. The Egyptian ruler initially relented, but when he chased after the departing Israelites Moses miraculously parted the Red Sea, allowing the Hebrews safe passage, and then allowed it to close in on the Egyptians, drowning their forces.

According to the Bible, 600,000 men left Egypt, plus women and children. When the Israelites were thirsty, Moses struck a rock to obtain water. And at times of hunger, God sent manna from heaven. Throughout they were attacked by poisonous snakes and hostile tribes, and were destabilized by bickering. One famous episode from the Israelites' time in the wilderness is Moses' ascent to the top of Mount Sinai to receive the tablets bearing the Ten Commandments. The tablets were later housed in the Ark of the Covenant, which resided in the Tabernacle.

Moses himself was not allowed to cross the River Jordan and so never entered the Promised Land, Canaan. According to the Bible, God himself buried the prophet when he died.

LA SECONDE PLAIE EN EGYPTE.

Die zweyte Egyptische Plage.

La Seconde Plaie en Egypte.

Und der Herr sprach zu Mose: sage Aaron: recke deine Hand aus mit deinem Stabe über die Bäche u. Ströme u. Brünne und Frösche über Egyptenland bringen. Und Aaron recket seine Hand über die Wasser in Egypten und kamen Frösche herauf, das Egyptenland bedeckt ward. und sie kamen in das Hauß, Kamer Lager und auf das Bette Pharao, in die Häußer seiner Knechte, unter sein Volck, in ihre Backöffen, und in ihre Teige. 2. Buch Mose Cap. 8. v. 3.5.6.

L'Eternel donc dit a Moise di a Aaron, eten ta main avec ta verge sur les fleuves, sur les rivieres, et sur les marais et fait monter les grenouilles sur la pais d'Egypte. Et ils sont monte dans la Maison, dans la Chambre et sur lit du Pharaon, et dans la Maison de ses serviteurs, et parmi tout son peuple, dans ses fours et dans leurs mais. Exode Cap. 8. v. 3.5.6.

OPPOSITE *The Israelites are guided by God in the form of a pillar of smoke.*
ABOVE *The second plague on Egypt, in which frogs overran the land.*

倣孫悟空

Journey to the West

In the 7th century the Chinese Buddhist monk Xuanzang made a legendary journey to India to obtain sacred texts. Nine centuries later, in the middle of the 16th century, the Chinese author Wu Cheng'en rewrote the story and introduced many fantastical elements.

In this mythical version, Xuanzang (also called Tripitaka) is accompanied on his quest by the supernatural Monkey King. Monkey is sent as a condition of being freed from prison, for he had caused chaos on earth and in heaven and hell; he had stolen the wand of the Dragon King of the Eastern Sea, removed his own pages from the *Register of the Living and the Dead*, and eaten the Peaches of Immortality that he was guarding. Xuanzang's

other two companions, Pigsy and Brother Sand, had also offended the gods.

On the journey the four characters encounter demons, hostile peoples, evil wizards, impassable rivers and out-of-control monsters. They arrive safely in India, however; and after obtaining *sutras* from the Buddha himself, Xuanzang and Monkey obtain buddhahood, while the other travellers are given celestial roles.

OPPOSITE *The mischievous Monkey examines a scroll.* ABOVE *Various exploits of the four explorers, as depicted by Hokusai.*

Into the Underworld

Heroes who descend into the underworld – the realm of the dead – and return are common to most mythologies. The Maya Hero Twins made the journey; upon their arrival, they challenged the lords of the underworld to a ball game (and won). In Norse mythology the semi-divine Hermod descends into Hel to retrieve Balder. Ancient Greek myth describes how Orpheus entered Hades to retrieve his beloved Eurydice; she was allowed to leave, but Orpheus was not permitted to look back until he was outside. He was unable to resist, however, and Eurydice was condemned to stay there for ever.

In the *Epic of Gilgamesh*, the wild Enkidu descends into the underworld, but – just like Orpheus – disobeys strict instructions and must remain there. However, the sun god Shamash creates a hole in the earth for Enkidu to escape.

Christ's descent into hell took place in the three days following his crucifixion. He released all those who had died up to that point, beginning with Adam, the first man. In Japan the first man, Izanagi, followed his wife Izanami into the underworld, but she chased him out. When he left, he gave birth to Amaterasu from his left eye.

The Finnish *Kalevala* epic contains the story of the hero Lemminkäinen. When he drowns in the river of the underworld, his mother searches high and low for him. Learning of his fate, she descends to the underworld, sews the pieces of his body back together, and with the help of the gods brings him back to life.

BELOW *The Cumaean Sibyl leads the Roman hero Aeneas through the underworld.* OPPOSITE *Dante and Virgil cross the River Acheron, in hell.*

The Holy Grail

The legend of the Holy Grail concerns the goblet used by Christ during the Last Supper, which supposedly had magical properties. Although grail legends seem to date from the 12th century, they may reflect earlier Celtic mythologies.

The best-known grail myths revolve around the court of King Arthur, specifically around the figure of Percival (sometimes called Parsifal). In a work by the French poet Chrétien de Troyes, written at the end of the 12th century, Percival sees the grail in a dream while staying at the magical residence of the Fisher King.

Other versions of the myth link the Grail closely with Sir Galahad. When Galahad is first introduced to Arthur's court, he sits in 'Siege Perilous' – the seat reserved for the knight who would discover the Grail. Galahad sets off on his quest, crossing the sea to a castle where the treasure is guarded by King Pelles. But Galahad is later transported to heaven by angels, and the Holy Grail is lost once more.

ABOVE *The Temple of the Holy Grail, as imagined by a German artist. The central male figure is Percival (Parsifal).* OPPOSITE *Arthur and his knights, seated at the Round Table, venerate the Holy Grail.*

t le roy fut issus du moustier et il bint
sais en hault si comanda q les nappes
itmises Et lors sallerent seoir les com
mons chm en son lieu ainsi come il auo
fait au matin Et quant ilz se furent to
lors oyrent ung estoy detonnaire si
t et si merueilleux quil lenr su aduis q

leu ne dive mot tant furent meuz grans
petis Et quant demon ves furet quat pierr
telle maniere que nul denlx nauoit pouoir
puoler ains regardoient to toe bestes mue

OVERVIEW OF WORLD MYTHOLOGIES

Australian Aboriginal Mythology

The indigenous people of Australia have inhabited that vast continent for around 50,000 years, and until relatively recently were largely cut off from other cultures. For this reason their mythology is closely related to the geography of Australia. As is also the case in Native American culture, some myths are shared between the different Aboriginal groups (of which there are several hundred), while others are specific to local topography and conditions.

For Aboriginal Australians, everything leads back to the Dreaming or Dreamtime – the time when the earth was formed. During this period the land was inhabited by spirits, or ancestors, who went on 'walkabouts'. As they travelled through the country, they created people and landmarks, as well as instigating ritual and ceremony. Although similar beliefs are found throughout Australia, stories relating to the creators tend to be localized. As in North America, the landscape is held to be sacred, and the source of life. Waterholes, caves and mountains, as well as landmarks such as Uluru (Ayers Rock), hold special significance, not least because many of them are seen as the remains of the creator beings themselves.

Key pan-Aboriginal figures include the so-called 'Rainbow Snake', a giant serpent that went about the land naming objects and creating landmarks. Another mythology has grown up around the character of Captain James Cook, the British sailor who 'discovered' Australia and who, for indigenous Australians, is depicted as something of a villain.

Celtic Mythology

The Celts were an Iron Age people found across Central Europe, northern Spain, France and the British Isles. The first signs of their culture date from the 8th century BC, though they had existed for millennia before this. Their polytheistic religion was widespread throughout Europe before Christianization: one particular branch, popular in Gaul and the British Isles, was Druidism.

The Celts had very little written culture. What we know today as 'Celtic' mythology comes mostly from Scotland, Ireland and Wales; most of these stories were first written down only in the 7th and 8th centuries AD, with many of the surviving documents dating from the 12th century. Happily for posterity, the Celts' principal enemy in the 1st century BC, Julius Caesar, wrote a history of his campaigns in Gaul, in which he described elements of their religion. Despite the fact that the Celts, the Romans and the Germanic tribes shared a common Indo-European heritage, Caesar probably went too far in relating Celtic gods to their Roman counterparts.

The main Celtic gods were Belenus (a solar god), Sulis (goddess of springs, and possibly an important mother goddess), Teutates (god of war), Lugus (the equivalent of Mercury, and god of the arts), Cernunnos (a horned fertility god) and Taranis (a Jupiter-like god of thunder). Taranis' symbol, a spoked wheel, appears often in Celtic art, as on the Gundestrup Cauldron.

In general terms, Celtic mythology is characterized by the importance and vitality of nature, the presence of a Great Goddess (and other powerful goddesses), and the existence of *genii loci* – spirits of a particular place.

Key texts: There are no surviving Celtic texts, but the Welsh *Mabinogion* epic gives a flavour of Celtic mythology, as do the Irish *Mythological* and *Fenian* cycles.

Central and South American Mythology

The most important civilizations of Mesoamerica were the Olmec (2nd millennium BC – c. 400 BC), the Maya (Classic period: AD 250–900), the Toltec (AD 800–1000) and the Aztec (14th–16th centuries AD). They flourished in the area more or less occupied by modern-day Mexico. Each was polytheistic, built pyramids, took an interest in the stars, and believed their capital to be the centre of the universe. They also shared a complex calendar. Most of them indulged in human sacrifice, regarding it as essential to the smooth running of the cosmos and to ensure that the gods provided water and sunlight.

Of the four civilizations, least is known about the Olmec, who had a series of gods that combined human and animal qualities. They left no writings, but it is assumed that their gods survived in the later cultures. Maya mythology, on the other hand, is known through the text called the *Popol Vuh*, which includes some of the stories relating to the Hero Twins and the origins of the sun and the moon. Both the Maya and the Aztec believed in personified forces of nature, and developed a cyclical theory of time, believing in a three-tiered universe and a nine-tiered underworld (the Maya referred to it as Xibalba, or 'fearful place').

Central to Maya mythology were the Hero Twins: culture heroes who had descended into Xibalba and defeated the lords of the underworld in a ball game, and who eventually turned themselves into the sun and the moon. The *Popol Vuh* tells their story and explains how the world was created, using the agricultural metaphor of maize (a staple of Mesoamerican culture), and how the creator Hurricane destroyed the first, defective humans with a flood. An imposter, Seven Macaw, attempted to take over as principal deity following this disaster, but was destroyed by the Hero Twins. Eventually humans were remade using maize.

Aztec mythology is known from the Aztecs' own codices and from accounts written by the Spanish *conquistadores*. The Aztec culture was centred on the city of Tenochtitlan, which was constructed from AD 1325 and which was thought by its creators to be the centre of the world. The Aztecs' underworld was called Mictlan, and their heaven Tlalocan. The human level in between was sustained by the sun. Suns were born and died in a cycle of renewal: the details vary according to different versions of the myth, but we are now in the age of the fifth sun, ruled over by Tonatiuh. The main Aztec gods are Quetzalcoatl (the Feathered Serpent, a creator god associated with water and rain, inherited from earlier cultures), Tezcatlipoca (a god of war) and Coatlicue (the serpent-skirted Great Mother).

The best-known pre-Columbian people of South America were the Inca, who occupied the Andes between the 12th century AD and the arrival of the Spanish in 1532. Their civilization was founded by the king Manco Capac, who some claimed was the son of the sun god Inti. For the Inca, the world was centred on the imperial capital of Cuzco, and the surrounding topography greatly influenced their mythology. Lake Titicaca was particularly sacred, being a *huaca*, a site or object of special significance. Like the Mesoamericans, the Incas believed in a three-tier world, a heaven and an underworld. Their main gods included Pacha Camac (the creator god), Viracocha (the bringer of civilization), Mama Cocha (the sea goddess) and Inti (the sun god).

Key text: The *Popol Vuh*.

Chinese, Japanese and Korean Mythology

The mythologies of China, Japan and Korea have all been deeply influenced by Buddhism, and each represents a synthesis of Buddhism with another belief system: Taoism in the case of China; Shintoism in Japan; and indigenous shamanistic beliefs in Korea.

Nonetheless, the three countries share many traditions. Each blurs the line between the real and the mythical – for example, in the way that earthly rulers are said to be descended from divinities. All feature a large collection of mythological creatures, chief among them the dragon. And all three give great significance to the cardinal directions (north, south, east, west), as well as to mountains, which are typically the homes of gods and spirits.

For the Koreans, humanity was preceded by proto-humans, who sinned by eating other living things (grapes), and so fell from grace, losing their immortality. To a certain extent they were redeemed by their first ruler, Hwanung (possibly descended from heaven), who taught them agriculture and other skills essential to life. According to one myth, Hwanung allowed a bear to become human: the bear, transformed into a beautiful woman, gave birth to Dangun, who in turn fathered the Korean people.

According to Chinese mythology, the creation began with Pan Gu, who separated earth from heaven. However, Taoism's highest deities are the Three Pure Ones, who embody the tao – creative flow – of the universe. They have come to be identified as Pan, Fu and Hu and Hua, who are also associated with the sky, the earth and the underworld. The whole of creation was presided over by the Jade Emperor (Yu Huang), an assistant of the Three Pure Ones.

Humanity's ultimate progenitors are often cited as Nuwa and Fuxi. Nuwa, who had a snake's body, created man. She also mended one of the four poles (possibly a mountain) that supported heaven after it had been hit by the demon Gong Gong. She repaired the damage by replacing the pole with the legs of a giant tortoise. Fuxi, Nuwa's brother and husband, went on to become one of the first rulers of China, followed by Shennong and Huang Di. Each of these figures, who are reputed to have lived in the 3rd millennium BC, taught their subjects the skills they needed to survive, including farming and medicine. The most important Chinese mythical beast is undoubtedly the dragon, which was believed to have power over the waters.

Japanese mythology combines folk beliefs with Buddhism and Shintoism. The Japanese pantheon is vast: even the current Japanese emperor is believed by some to be descended from the sun. The last of the earliest gods, Izanagi and Izanami, created the Japanese archipelago, with Izanami giving birth to eight of the islands. She was also mother to a number of minor gods, and was killed while giving birth to the incarnation of fire. Izanagi descended into hell to rescue his wife, but was unsuccessful. Upon returning, he created the gods Amaterasu and Susanoo, respectively the sun and storms. Amaterasu eventually gave her grandson, Ninigi, the Three Sacred Treasures, two of which still exist in holy places today. Japan's first emperor, Jimmu, was Ninigi's great-grandchild, and all subsequent emperors are traditionally held to be his descendants.

Hell appears often in Japanese art, with demons playing an important role in punishing and terrifying humanity. They form part of the wider body of monsters and spirits that people Japanese folk mythology.

Key texts: For Chinese mythology, the *Shan Hai Jing* ('Collection of the Mountains and Seas', written in the 2nd century BC), the *Hei'an Zhuan* ('Epic of Darkness', a record of oral tradition), and the *Journey to the West*. In Japan, the best compendiums are the *Kojiki* (a collection of myths from the 8th century AD) and the *Nihon Shoki* (finished in AD 720).

Egyptian Mythology

Ancient Egyptian mythology and society were shaped by the country's geography and climate – above all by the distinction between the two fertile slivers of land that flank the Nile and hostile desert. The Nile's annual flooding made agriculture possible – a crucial role that is reflected in Egyptian mythology.

The ancient Egyptian civilization endured from the 4th to the 1st millennium BC. What we know about its mythology comes from funerary art, inscriptions found on ancient monuments, fragments of the Book of the Dead, and Greek and Roman accounts. Central to Egyptian myth was the story of Isis and Osiris: Osiris was killed by his jealous brother Seth (who later became associated with chaos and evil), only to be resurrected by Isis, his sister and wife, long enough to conceive Horus. Osiris then descended into the underworld to become ruler of the dead. Osiris's death and rebirth reflects the annual flooding of the Nile.

Egyptian mythology also recognized the central importance of the sun god, Ra, who sailed around the world in a solar barque. His energies were renewed by Osiris, and every night he fought against Apep, a serpent of chaos; daybreak symbolized the restoration of order. Sometimes Apep would win their struggles, leading to thunderstorms. When Apep swallowed Ra whole, it resulted in solar eclipses.

Devotion cults were sometimes local and over time merged to create new deities. As in Mesopotamia, Egyptian gods could often have political meaning, and new pharaohs could chose to emphasize the importance of a particular deity. For example, the creation myth that emerged in Heliopolis held that Atum (who created himself from the waters of chaos) was the creator of the world. Later he was conflated with Ra to create Atum-Ra.

Other key gods include Thoth (the 'heart of Ra', associated with the moon, time and magic), Anubis (the jackal-headed funerary god), Bes (a household god), Geb (the earth god), Nut (the sky goddess) and Hathor (the cow sky goddess).

Key texts: The Book of the Dead; Plutarch's 'On Isis and Osiris'; Herodotus' *Histories*, Book 2.

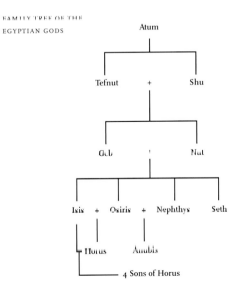

FAMILY TREE OF THE
EGYPTIAN GODS

Greek and Roman Mythology

Europe's best-known mythological system, and the basis of much religion between the 2nd millennium BC and the 5th century AD, Greek and Roman myth is bursting with tales that have been told and retold hundreds of times. All readers will be familiar with the stories of Theseus and the Minotaur, Odysseus, the Trojan Horse, Heracles' labours, and Romulus and Remus. And many will be familiar with the stories of endless bickering and romance between the gods and mortals (Zeus's romantic conquests, for instance), with Ovid's *Metamorphoses*, or Jason's quest for the Golden Fleece. We know these myths not only from texts, but also from a huge number of artworks, including sculpture and (in the case of Greek mythology) painted vases.

The first generation of gods in Greek mythology are primeval beings without concrete form. They include Chaos, Eros and Gaia (Earth), and are rarely depicted in art. These deities in turn gave birth to the Titans (as well as to a range of monsters), two of whom – Cronus and Rhea – were the parents of Zeus and his siblings. In time, Zeus overthrew his father, leading to the dominance of the Olympians, the 'classic' pantheon of twelve main gods (Zeus, Hera, Poseidon, Demeter, Athena, Dionysus, Apollo, Artemis, Ares, Aphrodite, Hephaestus and Hermes). These were thereafter immortal and unchanging. However, between them (and with mortals) they fathered an astonishing range of other deities, demigods and other spirits – as well as humans themselves.

The origins of humanity are ascribed to various figures, including Zeus and Prometheus. Humankind then suffers a downward progression, through the Gold, Silver, Bronze, Heroic and Iron Ages. The Heroic Age is the age of the Trojan War, the axial event in Greek mythology. In this tale, told by Homer in the *Iliad* and the *Odyssey*, an alliance of Greek city-states sails to Troy to take back the abducted Helen, resulting in a ten-year conflict in which the gods also took sides. Thereafter, the *Odyssey* tells of Odysseus' return home.

Overall, the Greek view of the world is one suffused with magic, in which anything might happen (even to gods) and in which forms are deceptive and ever changing. A common trope is that of the hero battling a monster, such as Theseus and the Minotaur, Jason and the Dragon, Oedipus and the Sphinx, or Heracles and the Hydra.

The essentials of Roman mythology often differ from Greek mythology only in name: Zeus becomes Jupiter, Ares becomes Mars, Hera becomes Juno, Aphrodite becomes Venus, and so on. However, there were some important innovations, and Roman versions of the Greek gods sometimes also incorporated elements from the religion of the earlier Etruscans. Roman mythology was also influenced by the Romans' far-flung conquests, which led to the adoption of various deities from other regions: the cult of Cybele, for example, was an influential import from the Near East. The foundation myth of Rome – the story of Romulus and Remus – was of course specific to the empire; nonetheless, the emperor Augustus commissioned Virgil to compose the *Aeneid*, in which the poet traced Rome's origins back to the Trojan prince Aeneas. According to this version of events, Aeneas escaped Troy at the time of the Greeks' victory, sailed around the Mediterranean for several years (in the style of Odysseus) and eventually ended up in Italy, where his son founded Rome.

It seems that Greco-Roman mythology later influenced Celtic and probably also Norse myth, notably in the pantheon's domination by the thunder god (Zeus/Jupiter, Taranis or Thor).

Key texts: Hesiod's *Theogony*; Homer's *Iliad* and *Odyssey*; Ovid's *Metamorphoses*; Virgil's *Aeneid*.

FAMILY TREE OF THE GREEK GODS

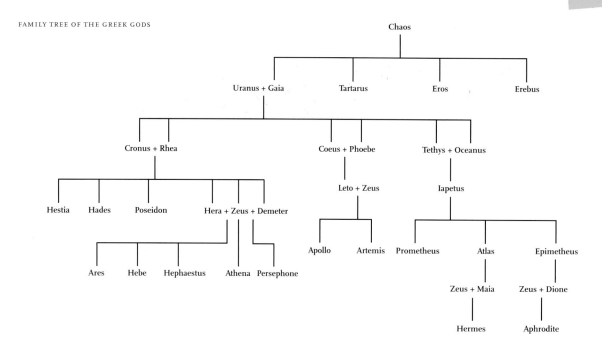

Hindu Mythology

Hinduism is practised principally in modern-day India and Bali. It stems from the religion of the Vedic period, which is based on four divinely revealed texts called the Vedas, dating as far back as the 2nd millennium BC.

The Vedas describe various creation myths, including the myth of Purusha, the first man, who was dismembered to form the entire universe, including the gods. Another origin myth tells of a golden egg from which creation burst forth. Nevertheless, creation is cyclical, forever reinventing itself over spectacularly long periods.

Effectively there are three principal gods in Hinduism: Brahma (the Creator), Vishnu (the Sustainer) and Shiva (the Destroyer). Each can have many avatars and alternate forms, allowing them to appear in different scenarios; in many respects they are all aspects of Brahman, the single, divine consciousness. The three main gods each have a consort (Lakshmi, Parvati and Saraswati, respectively), and each consort also has several avatars, including the figures of Durga and Kali. There are also less important, but still popular, gods, including Agni, the god of fire, and the elephant-headed Ganesha. Overall, the gods' roles are less rigid than in Greek mythology. On the side of evil are the *asuras*, a type of demon, although even they can be surprisingly pious.

Within this massive, overarching framework are various stand out events. for example, the Churning of the Ocean of Milk, which the gods and demons undertook between them to obtain the elixir of immortality. During this task Lakshmi, the goddess of good fortune and light, emerged; she is celebrated today in the feast of Diwali. Another story tells of a flood that covered the earth, which was then rescued by Vishnu in the form of a giant boar that pushed the earth up.

There are two key epics in Hinduism: the *Ramayana* and the *Mahabharata*. The latter, which contains the famous, instructive *Bhagavad Gita*, tells the story of a war between two families, essentially a conflict between good and evil. The outcome of the final battle at Kurukshetra is determined by Krishna (an avatar of Vishnu), just as the Greek gods had been decisive at Troy.

Key texts: The collection of writings known as the Vedas, as well as the *Mahabharata* and *Ramayana*.

Judaeo-Christian Mythology

Owing to their geographical origins in the Near East, the traditions of Judaism and Christianity are both heavily influenced by Egyptian, Mesopotamian, Greek, Canaanite and Persian mythologies. Like Islam, to which they are related, both are still active religions.

The biblical Old Testament describes how the earth and the universe were created, and how the earth was populated. It includes an early clash between good and evil in the story of Adam and Eve, as well as between their sons, Cain and Abel. Within a few generations God was disappointed by his creation, and decided to destroy all of humanity except for Noah and his family. The Old Testament also accounts for the rise of different languages (the story of the Tower of Babel) and explains why humans die at a particular age; it also sets down laws, in the form of the Ten Commandments. Among its many stories, one which tells of the journey of the Jews in Egypt, and their struggle to reach their Promised Land under the guidance of Moses.

The Christian New Testament tells the story of Jesus Christ, an archetypal hero figure. Born to the Virgin Mary, he performed a range of miracles (walking on water, raising the dead, turning water into wine). He ultimately sacrificed himself through his crucifixion, in order to absolve humanity of its sin, before coming back to life and ascending into heaven. According to some traditions, before his resurrection he descended into the underworld to release the souls of those who had died in earlier times.

The traditional Christian conception of the universe has three tiers: the mortal world, with heaven above and hell below. Hell is ruled over by Satan, a fallen angel who later tempted Christ. The New Testament closes with St John of Patmos's vision of the end of the world, which includes the final defeat of Satan and the Final Judgment of the living and the dead.

Post-biblical mythology centres on the legends of saints, some of whom perform miracles or do battle against monsters – including, for example, St George.

Key texts: The Bible; Jacobus de Voragine's *The Golden Legend*.

Mesopotamian Mythology

The term Mesopotamia refers to the land between the Euphrates and Tigris rivers in modern-day Iraq, and a civilization that began there over 5,000 years ago. The region's traditions encompass Akkadian, Babylonian, Sumerian, Assyrian and, to some extent, Hittite mythology. There is great regional variation in terms of gods, names of gods and stories, but in general the heavens reflect the political organization on earth, and certain gods are tied to a particular city. Many gods are ambiguous in their spheres of influence: the storm and air god Enlil, for example, also controlled fertility.

According to the Akkadian *Enuma Elish*, in the beginning there were only the male Apsu (fresh water) and the female Tiamat (also known as Nammu; salt water). Together, they created the elements of the world, but they also fought. Apsu was eventually overcome, while Tiamat and her monstrous army was challenged and overcome by the king-god Marduk. Marduk then became the first king, a triumph of order over chaos. Tiamat's body was split up to create the earth and the sky. And Marduk's new capital was called Babylon.

In other regional creation myths credit for creating the universe is given to the freshwater god Enki (the Akkadian name for Ea), who after creating the different parts of the world gave each to a minor god. Then, through a series of incestuous couplings, including one with the mother goddess Ninhursaga, the world came into being. Enki's virility is a metaphor for the life-giving qualities of water. Humans were created to do the work of the gods, and to give them unlimited leisure.

However, the much later *Epic of Gilgamesh* tells how Enki/Ea tired of humanity and their ceaseless noise, and decided to destroy the world in a flood. One man, Utnapishtim, was chosen to be saved.

Later Persian mythology, which influenced the Zoroastrian religion, differed significantly, and centred on the figures of Ahura Mazda (good, light) and Ahriman (darkness). In the Zoroastrian pantheon, perhaps the best-known god is Mithra, a god of covenants who was later conflated with the Roman god Apollo. Perhaps the best-known collection of Persian mythology is the *Shahnama*, from about AD 1000, which contains the legend of the hero Rostam.

Key texts: The *Epic of Gilgamesh* is one of the world's first epic and tells the tale of the hero Gilgamesh and his quest for immortality. See also the *Enuma Elish*. For Persian legend, the *Shahnama* is an excellent compendium.

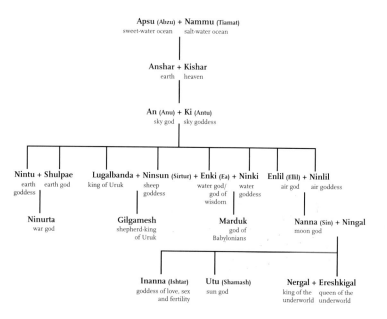

Norse Mythology

Until the 11th century AD, when it was replaced by Christianity, the Norse belief system could be found across the north of Europe, from the Angles, Saxons, Danes and Jutes, to the Norwegians, Swedes and the people of Iceland. In fact, it is difficult to distinguish the Norse pantheon from a more general 'Germanic' one.

According to Norse mythology, the universe comprised nine worlds, of which the most important (for humans) is Midgard, the world of day-to-day experience. Midgard is surrounded by a sea inhabited by the Midgard Serpent. These nine worlds are arranged around the World Tree, Yggdrasil.

The head of the principal gods, who were known collectively as the Aesir, was Odin, who lived at Valhalla. Other key deities included Thor (Odin's son), Loki, Freyr and Balder. Loki, although a god, gave birth to various monsters, and often betrayed or played tricks on the gods. The forces of chaos were represented by the Frost Giants, who struggled against the Aesir. There was also a second race of gods, the Vanir, but their mythological profile is less significant.

Norse mythology is ruled by prophecy. Odin, for example, was terrified of a prophecy that he would be devoured by the giant wolf Fenrir, leading him to raise an army of dead soldiers. The destruction of the gods is seen as inevitable: during Ragnarok ('doom of the gods'), everybody will converge to fight to the death. The flaming earth will sink into the sea, but will be reborn, governed by the good god Balder.

Key texts: The *Poetic Edda* and the *Prose Edda*, the latter by the Icelandic historian Snorri Sturluson, gather together various earlier myths.

Native American Mythology

Throughout North America, from Texas to Canada, Native American mythology reflects the separate traditions of hundreds of tribes – Hopi, Sioux, Navajo and Cherokee, to name but a few – who once occupied the land. For non-Native Americans, the main obstacle to an understanding of this mythology is the lack of written texts.

Nevertheless, it is possible to detect some common elements. Native American mythology places great emphasis on the role of nature, and reflects the belief that all things – even rocks and rivers – have a spirit. Nature is sacred, and the landscape is dotted with holy places – springs, mountains, river, canyons – that have particular significance. Animals are seen as the ancestors of humans.

Native American cosmological myths tend to assume that the universe originated from the waters, and many tribes have earth-diver stories, in which some humble creature brings land to the surface little by little. In other traditions, the role of creator is given to the Spider Grandmother, who ushered people from a previous world into the current world (the existence of multiple worlds is a common feature of Native American myths). It is telling that the principal gods – typically the Sky Father and the Earth Mother – rarely feature, even in creation myths: they often seem very removed from day-to-day life.

Native American mythology is notable for its large number of tricksters, principal among them Raven and Coyote. These sometimes comical, sometimes almost evil characters enjoy turning things on their head, and are frequently highly sexual. Their popularity has made them the protagonists of many adventures.

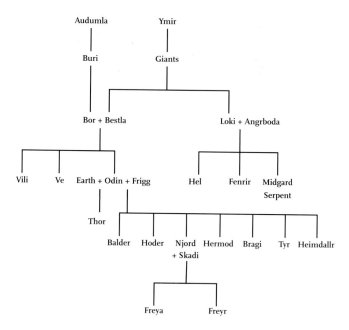

FURTHER READING

Just as myths can vary widely, even within a single culture, so too can interpretations. The following list consists of publications, from story books to academic studies, that offer a range of different viewpoints.

GENERAL

Robert Adkinson, *Sacred Symbols: Peoples, Religions, Mysteries*. London: Thames & Hudson, 2009
Karen Armstrong, *A Short History of Myth*, Edinburgh: Canongate, 2006
Joseph Campbell, *The Hero with a Thousand Faces*, Princeton, N.J.: Princeton University Press, 2004
Christopher Dell, *Monsters: A Bestiary of the Bizarre*, London: Thames & Hudson, 2010
William G. Doty (ed.), *World Mythology: Myths and Legends of the World Brought to Life*, New York: Barnes & Noble, 2002
Geoffrey Kirk, *Myth: Its Meaning and Function in Ancient and Other Cultures*, Berkeley, Calif.: 1970
David Leeming, *The Oxford Companion to World Mythology*, Oxford: Oxford University Press, 2005
C. Scott Littleton (ed.), *Mythology: The Illustrated Anthology of World Myth and Storytelling*, London: Duncan Baird, 2002
Jaan Puhvel, *Comparative Mythology*, Baltimore: John Hopkins University Press, 1989
Lewis Spence, *Introduction to Mythology*, Guernsey: Studio Editions, 1994

AFRICAN MYTHOLOGY

Stephen Belcher (ed.), *African Myths of Origin*, London: Penguin, 2005
Harold Courlander, *Tales of Yoruba: Gods and Heroes*, New York: Original Publications, 1995
Baba Ifa Karade, *The Handbook of Yoruba Religious Concepts*, York Beach, Me.: Weiser, 1994
Patricia Ann Lynch and Jeremy Roberts, *African Mythology, A to Z*, Chelsea House Publishers, 2010
Ngangur Mbitu and Ranchor Prime, *Essential African Mythology: Stories That Change the World*, London: Thorsons, 1997
Harold Scheub, *A Dictionary of African Mythology*, New York: Oxford University Press, 2000

CELTIC MYTHOLOGY

Peter Berresford Ellis, *The Mammoth Book of Celtic Myths and Legends*, London: Robinson, 2002
Arthur Cotterell, *Mythology of the Celts: Myths and Legends of the Celtic World*, London: Southwater, 2007
Miranda Green, *Animals in Celtic Life and Myth*, London: Routledge, 1992
Miranda J. Green, *Dictionary of Celtic Myth and Legend*, London: Thames & Hudson, 1992
Simon James, *Exploring the World of the Celts*, London: Thames & Hudson, 2005

The Mabinogion, trans. Sioned Davies, New York and Oxford: Oxford University Press, 2008
James MacKillop, *Dictionary of Celtic Mythology*, Oxford: Oxford University Press, 1998
John Matthews, *The Grail: Quest for the Eternal*, London: Thames & Hudson, 1981
Christopher Snyder, *Exploring the World of King Arthur*, London: Thames & Hudson, 2011

CENTRAL AND SOUTH AMERICAN MYTHOLOGY

K. Berrin and E. Pasztory (eds.), *Teotihuacan: Art from the City of the Gods*, London: Thames & Hudson, 1993
David M. Jones, *Mythology of the Aztecs and Maya*, London: Southwater, 2007
Mary Ellen Miller and Karl Taube, *An Illustrated Dictionary of the Gods and Symbols of Ancient Mexico and the Maya*, London: Thames & Hudson, 1997
Popol Vuh, trans. Dennis Tedlock, New York: Simon & Schuster, 1996
Paul Richard Steele, *Handbook of Inca Mythology*, Santa Barbara, Calif.: ABC-CLIO, 2004
Karl Taube, *Aztec and Maya Myths*, Austin, Tex.: University of Texas Press, 1993

EAST ASIAN MYTHOLOGY

Michael Ashkenazi, *Handbook of Japanese Mythology*, New York: Oxford University Press, 2008
Anne M. Birrell, *Chinese Mythology: An Introduction*, Baltimore and London: Johns Hopkins University Press, 1999
Manchao Cheng, *The Origin of Chinese Deities*, Beijing: Foreign Language Press, 1995
F. Hadland Davis, *Myths and Legends of Japan*, New York: Dover Publications, 1992
P.-G. Hwang, *Korean Myths and Folk Legends*, Fremont, Calif.: Jain Publishing, 2006
David Leeming, *A Dictionary of Asian Mythology*, Oxford: Oxford University Press, 2001
M. Lewis, *The Flood Myths of Early China*, Albany, N.Y.: State University of New York Press, 2006
Keith G. Stevens, *Chinese Mythological Gods*, New York: Oxford University Press, 2000
Lihui Yang, Deming An and Jessica Anderson Turner, *Handbook of Chinese Mythology (Handbooks of World Mythology)*, New York: Oxford University Press, 2008
Hiroko Yoda and Matt Alt, *Yokai Attack!: The Japanese Monster Survival Guide*, Tokyo: Kodansha International, 2008
Wu Ch'eng'en, *Monkey*, trans. Arthur Waley, London: Penguin, 2005

EGYPTIAN MYTHOLOGY

The Egyptian Book of the Dead, trans. E. A. Wallis Budge, London: Penguin, 2008
G. Hart, *Egyptian Myths*, London: British Museum Press, 1990

Manfred Lurker, *An Illustrated Dictionary of the Gods and Symbols of Ancient Egypt*, London: Thames & Hudson, 1982
Geraldine Pinch, *Egyptian Mythology: A Guide to the Gods, Goddesses, and Traditions of Ancient Egypt*, New York: Oxford University Press, 2004
Joyce Tyldesley, *The Penguin Book of Myths and Legends of Ancient Egypt*, London: Penguin, 2010
Richard H. Wilkinson, *The Complete Gods and Goddesses of Ancient Egypt*, London: Thames & Hudson, 2003

GREEK AND ROMAN MYTHOLOGY

Lucilla Burn, *Greek Myths*, London: British Museum Press, 1990
Richard Buxton, *Imaginary Greece: The Contexts of Mythology*, Cambridge: Cambridge University Press, 1994
Richard Buxton, *The Complete World of Greek Mythology*, London: Thames & Hudson, 2004
Malcolm Day, *100 Characters from Classical Mythology*, New York: Barron's, 2007
Hesiod, *Theogony and Works and Days*, trans. M. L. West, London: Penguin, 2008
Homer, *The Iliad*, trans. E. V. Rieu, London and New York: Penguin, 2003
Homer, *The Odyssey*, trans. E. V. Rieu, intro. Peter Jones, London and New York: Penguin, 2006
C. Kerényi, *The Gods of the Greeks*, London: Thames & Hudson, 1951
C. Kerényi, *The Heroes of the Greeks*, London: Thames & Hudson, 1997
Stephen P. Kershaw, *The Greek Myths: Gods, Monsters, Heroes and the Origins of Storytelling*, London: Robinson, 2007
Philip Matyszak, *The Greek and Roman Myths: A Guide to the Classical Stories*, London: Thames & Hudson, 2010
Ovid, *Metamorphoses*, trans. David Raeburn, London: Penguin, 2004
Barry B. Powell, *Classical Myth*, Boston, Mass. and London: Pearson, 2012

HINDU AND INDIAN MYTHOLOGY

The Bhagavad Gita, trans. W. J. Johnson, Oxford: Oxford University Press, 2008
Yves Bonnefoy (ed.), *Asian Mythologies*, Chicago: University of Chicago Press, 1993
Anna L. Dallapiccola, *Dictionary of Hindu Lore and Legend*, London: Thames & Hudson, 2004
Wendy Doniger, *Hindu Myths: A Sourcebook Translated from the Sanskrit*, London: Penguin, 2004
John Dowson, *A Classical Dictionary of Hindu Mythology and Religion, Geography, History, and Literature*, London: Routledge, 2000
The Mahabharata, trans. John D. Smith, London: Penguin, 2009

JUDAEO-CHRISTIAN MYTHOLOGY

Bernard Frank Batto, *Slaying the Dragon: Mythmaking in the Biblical Tradition*,

Louisville, Ky.: John Knox Press, 1999
Norman Cohn, *Cosmos, Chaos, and the World to Come*, New Haven, Conn. and London: Yale University Press, 2001
Gary Greenberg, *101 Myths of the Bible: How Ancient Scribes Invented Biblical History*, Naperville, Il.: Sourcebooks, 2002
David Leeming, *Jealous Gods and Chosen People: The Mythology of the Middle East*, New York: Oxford University Press, 2004

MIDDLE EASTERN AND NEAR EASTERN MYTHOLOGY

Jeremy Black and Anthony Green, *Gods, Demons and Symbols of Ancient Mesopotamia*, London: British Museum Press, 1992
S. G. F. Brandon, *Creation Legends of the Ancient Near East*, London: Hodder and Stoughton, 1963
Stephanie Dalley, *Myths from Mesopotamia: Creation, The Flood, Gilgamesh, and Others*, Oxford: Oxford University Press, 2008
The Epic of Gilgamesh, trans. Andrew George, London: Penguin, 2003
Samuel Noah Kramer, *Sumerian Mythology: A Study of Spiritual and Literary Achievement in the Third Millennium BC*, Philadelphia: University of Pennsylvania Press, 1998
Diana Wolkstein and Samuel Noah Kramer, *Inanna, Queen of Heaven and Earth*, New York: Harper, 1983

NATIVE AMERICAN MYTHOLOGY

David Jones, *The Illustrated Encyclopedia of American Indian Mythology: Legends, Gods and Spirits of North, Central and South America*, Leicester: Anness, 2010
David Leeming and Jake Page, *Mythology of Native North America*, Norman, Okla.: University of Oklahoma Press, 2000
Alfonso Ortiz and Richard Erdoes, *American Indian Myths and Legends*, London: Pimlico, 1997
Alfonso Ortiz and Richard Erdoes, *American Indian Trickster Tales*, New York: Penguin, 1998
Zitkala-Sa, Cathy N. Davidson and Ada Norris, *American Indian Stories, Legends, and Other Writings*, London: Penguin, 2003

NORSE MYTHOLOGY

Margaret Clunies Ross, *Prolonged Echoes: Volume 1: Old Norse Myths in Medieval Northern Society*, Odense: University Press of Southern Denmark, 1995
H. R. Ellis Davidson, *Gods and Myths of Northern Europe*, Harmondsworth: Penguin, 1971
Carolyne Larrington (trans.), *The Poetic Edda*, Oxford: Oxford University Press, 1996
John Lindow, *Norse Mythology: A Guide to the Gods, Heroes, Rituals, and Beliefs*, Oxford: Oxford University Press, 2002

LIST OF ILLUSTRATIONS

a = above, b = below, c = centre, l = left, r = right

1 From O. v. Leixner, *Illustrirte Geschichte des deutschen Schriftthums*, vol. 1 (Leipzig and Berlin, 1880). Photo akg-images

2 Giovanni Domenico Tiepolo, *The Procession of the Trojan Horse into Troy*, c. 1760. National Gallery, London.

5l Bull's head, Mesopotamia, 3rd millennium BC. Musée du Louvre. Photo Marie-Lan Nguyen

5c Jade mask from Monte Alban, Mexico, 150 BC – AD 100. Museo Nacional de Antropología, Mexico City.

5r Double-headed serpent in turquoise mosaic, Mexico, 15th–16th centuries AD. British Museum, London.

6 The Moon and Jupiter meet in Sagittarius, manuscript from Cairo, c. 1250. Bibliothèque Nationale, Paris, Ms. Arabe 2583, fol. 26v.

7 Dante Gabriel Rossetti, *Pandora*, 1878. Lady Lever Art Gallery, Liverpool.

8a Attic red-figure cup painted by Onesimos, 500–490 BC. Musée du Louvre, Paris.

8b Fired clay statue of Xolotl, c. 1350–1521. Staatliche Museen zu Berlin. Werner Forman Archive/Museum für Volkerkunde, Berlin.

9a Amulet, late 6th–4th centuries BC. Musée du Louvre, Paris, Acc. Sb 3566. Photo Marie-Lan Nguyen.

9b The classical constellations, from the Codex Barberinianus Latinus 76, Italian, 15th century. Biblioteca Apostolica Vaticana, Rome.

10a Stained-glass window, 19th century. Canterbury Cathedral. Photo © Painton Cowen.

10b Thoth with a scribe, c. 1550–1295 BC. Werner Forman Archive/Egyptian Museum, Berlin.

11a 'The Ash Yggdrasil', from Wilhelm Wägner, *Asgard and the Gods* (London, 1886), p. 27.

11b Gundestrup Cauldron, 1st century BC. Nationalmuseet, Copenhagen.

12 Yama with the Samsara, Tibetan manuscript. Wellcome Library, London.

13a Hanuman carrying the Mountain to Lakshmana, Indian manuscript. Wellcome Library, London.

13b Vishnu (Beikthano in Burma) riding Garuda, from Richard Carnac Temple, *The Thirty-Seven Nats*, (London, 1906).

14–15 Francesco Botticini, *Assumption of the Virgin*, 1475–76. National Gallery, London.

16 Giulio Romano, *Olympus and Zeus Destroying the Rebellious Giants*, 1530–32. Palazzo del Te, Mantua.

17 Hendrick Goltzius, *Icarus* and *Phaethon*, 1588. Engravings.

18 Ceremonial staff, 19th–20th centuries. Werner Forman Archive/Musée Royal de l'Afrique Centrale, Tervuren.

19l Bronze bust of Cybele, 1st century AD. Cabinet des Médailles, Bibliotheque Nationale, Paris. Photo Marie-Lan Nguyen.

19r Bronze figurine of Baal, 14th–12th centuries BC. Louvre, Paris. Photo Marie-Lan Nguyen.

20l Pan Gu, from Wang Qi's *Sancai Tuhui*, c. 1607.

20r From E. A. Wallis Budge, *Studies in Egyptian Mythology* (London, 1904).

21 God as architect, mid- to late 13th century illumination. Cathedral Museum, Toledo.

22 Bernard Picart after Abraham Jansz van. Diepenbeeck, *The Chaos*, 1731. Engraving. Private collection/The Stapleton Collection/The Bridgeman Art Library.

23 Fragment of an Athenian vase, c. 400 BC. Museo Nazionale, Naples.

24 Jan van Kessel and Hendrik van Balen, *The Feast of the Gods*, c. 1600. Oil on canvas. Musee d'Art et d'Histoire, Saint-Germain-en-Laye. Giraudon/The Bridgeman Art Library.

25 Tapestry of animal gods, Tibet. Wellcome Library, London.

26 Saxon deities. Etching. Wellcome Library, London.

27 After David Roberts, *Egyptian deities at Abu Simbel, Egypt*, 1846. Coloured lithograph. Wellcome Library, London.

28 Sri Mariamman Temple, Singapore. World Religions Photo Library/The Bridgeman Art Library.

29 Japanese domestic shrine, 19th century. Wellcome Library, London.

30l Aztec 'sun stone'. National Museum of Anthropology, Mexico City. Photo Vincent Roux.

30r Head of Brahma, from Cambodia, 9th–10th centuries. Musée Guimet, Paris. Photo Vassil.

31 Brahma, Indian manuscript, 19th century. Wellcome Library, London.

32 J. Sadeler after Martin de Vos, *Jupiter in his Chariot*, c. 1595. Engraving. Wellcome Library, London.

33l Peter Paul Rubens, *Saturn Devouring Poseidon*, 1636–38. Museo del Prado, Madrid.

33r Michelangelo, *God Creating the Planets*, 1508–12. Sistine Chapel, Vatican, Rome.

34 Coatlicue sculpture, Aztec. National Museum of Anthropology, Mexico City. Photo Wolfgang Sauber.

35 Fresco from the Temple of Isis, Pompeii. National Archaeological Museum, Naples. Photo akg-images/Erich Lessing.

36l Ishtar holding a weapon, early 2nd millennium BC. Terracotta. Musée du Louvre, Paris. Photo Marie-Lan Nguyen.

36r Nuwa and Fuxi, 7th–10th centuries AD. Xinjiang Uighur Autonomous Region Museum.

37l 'Isis', from Athanasius Kircher, *Oedipus*, vol. 1 (Rome, 1662–64), p. 189.

37r Bernard van Orley, *Jupiter and Juno Govern the World*, tapestry, 16th century. Palacio Real, Madrid.

38l Johann Ulrich Kraus, 'Heaven', from the *Historische Bilder Bible* (Augsburg, 1700).

38r From John Thomson, *Illustrations of China and its People*, vol. 4 (London, 1873–74). Wellcome Library, London.

39 From E. Müller-Baden, *The Nine Worlds* (c. 1900). Photo akg-images.

40 Mural of a cosmic mandala from Songzanlin Monastery, Deqin, China, 17th century. Photo Monique Pietri/akg-images.

41 Jain cosmological map, 19th century. Wellcome Library, London.

42 Utagawa Kunisada, *Amaterasu Enticed from her Cave by Dancing Gods*, woodcut, 1857.

43 The sun, from a Persian manuscript, 17th–18th centuries. Wellcome Library, London.

44l Joseph Heintz the Elder, *The Fall of Phaethon*, 1596. Museum der bildenden Künste, Leipzig.

44a Gustave Moreau, *Phoebus and Boreas*, c. 1879. Musée Gustave Moreau, Paris.

44b Sol in his chariot, from Guido Bonatti, *Liber Astronomiae* (Augsburg, 1491).

45 Surya in his chariot. Gouache drawing. Wellcome Library, London.

46 Roman altar, 2nd century AD. Musée du Louvre, Paris. Photo Marie-Lan Nguyen.

47a Sacrificial stone from Tenochtitlan. Museo del Templo Mayor. Photo Vincent Roux.

47b Impression from a Mesopotamian seal, 1000–539 BC. Werner Forman Archive/British Museum, London.

48 Bronze mirror, Tang Dynasty. Honolulu Academy of Arts.

49 From Giovanni Battista Ferrari, *Flora, seu de florum cultura* (Amsterdam, 1646). Wellcome Library, London.

50l fol. 54r from the Codex Ríos (Codex Vaticanus Latinus A), c. 1570–95. Biblioteca Apostolica Vaticana, Rome.

50r From *Urania's Mirror* (London, c. 1825).

51 Armenian manuscript of a treatise on heavenly movements, c. 1795. Wellcome Library, London.

52l Byzantine diagram of the zodiac, 8th century. Biblioteca Apostolica Vaticana, Rome, Vat. gr. 1292, fol. 9.

52r Pottery tile, Han Dynasty. Musée Cernuschi, Paris. Photo Guillaume Jacquet.

53 Mosaic from a Roman villa in Sentinum (Umbria), c. AD 200–250. Glyptothek, Munich. Photo Bibi Saint-Pol.

54a From Emilie Kip Baker, *Stories from Northern Myths* (New York, 1914), facing p. 202.

54b Jacopo Tintoretto (attrib.), *Jupiter and Semele*, c. 1545. National Gallery, London.

55 Antonio da Correggio, *Jupiter and Io*, c. 1530. Kunsthistorisches Museum, Vienna.

56 Front panel of the Ludovisi Throne, c. 460 BC. Museo Nazionale Romano, Rome. Photo G. Dagli Orti/CORBIS.

57 Shiva and Parvati bathing, manuscript, early 19th century. Chandigarh Museum.

58 Maerten van Heemskerck, *Vulcan Showing the Captured Mars and Venus to the Gods*, c. 1536. Kunsthistorisches Museum, Vienna. Photo akg-images/Erich Lessing.

59 Vishnu and Lakshmi meet Shiva, Parvati and Ganesha. Chromolithograph. Wellcome Library, London.

60 Hokusai, *Two Gods*, woodcut, 19th century.

61 From the Madrid Codex (Codex Tro-Cortesianus), probably 17th century. Museo de América, Madrid.

62a Relief plaque from the Gundestrup Cauldron, 1st century AD. Nationalmuseet, Copenhagen. Photo akg-images/Erich Lessing.

62b Sandro Botticelli, *The Birth of Venus*, c. 1486. Galleria degli Uffizi, Florence.

63 Mårten Eskil Winge, *Thor's Battle with the Ettins*, 1872. Nationalmuseum, Stockholm.

64 Joseph Anton Koch, *Landscape with Noah*, c. 1803. Pinakothek, Munich.

65 Guy Head after Giovanni Folo, *Iris*, 1814. Engraving. Wellcome Library, London.

66 George Frederic Watts, *Uldra, The Scandinavian Spirit of the Rainbow in the Waterfall*, 1884. Private collection. Photo Bonhams, London/The Bridgeman Art Library.

67 William Gersham Collingwood, *The Northern Gods Descending*, 1890. Private collection. Photo Bonhams, London/The Bridgeman Art Library.

68 Attic water jar, c. 440–430 BC. Antikenmuseum Basel und Sammlung Ludwig, Basel.

69 Roman fresco from the House of the Vettii, Pompeii.

70l Eshu, Yoruba sculpture, Nigeria, 1881–1920. Science Museum, London/Wellcome Images.

70a 'Coyote', from Edward S. Curtis, *Indian Days of the Long Ago* (Yonkers-on-Hudson: World Book Company, 1915), p. 84.

70b 'The Birth of Maui', from Wilhelm Dittmer, *Te Tohunga* (London, 1907).

71 Louis Huard, 'The Punishment of Loki', from A. and E. Keary, *The Heroes of Asgard* (London: Macmillan, 1900).

72 Gustave Doré, 'Giants Chained in Hell', from Dante's *Inferno* (Paris, 1861), Plate LXV.

73 Luca Giordano, *The Boat of Charon, Sleep, Night and Morpheus*, 1684–86. Fresco. Palazzo Medici-Riccardi, Florence.

74a Ludvig Abelin Schou, 'Hel and the Valkyries', from P. Johansen, *Nordisk Oldtid og Dansk Kunst* (Copenhagen, 1907), p. 107.

74b Thomas Stothard after Francesco

INDEX

||||||||||||||||||||||

Page numbers in *italic* refer to illustrations.